To my good

Wm Loelnick.

COUNT YOURSELF IN

Wyn Lodwick's recordings

Y Band yn ei Le (vinyl)
Jazz o Gymru (cassette)
Y Cyswllt Cymraeg – Dill a Wyn (cassette & CD)
Pump Hewl i Harlem (cassette)
Wyn and Friends – 50 years of Jazz (CD)
Wyn Lodwick a'r Band – Wyn a'i Fyd (CD)

Count Yourself In

A Man and his Jazz

Wyn Lodwick

Trans:
Lyn Ebenezer

First published in 2010

© Author: Wyn Lodwick

© English translation: Lyn Ebenezer

© Gwasg Carreg Gwalch 2010

Published with the financial support
of the Welsh Books Council

ISBN: 978-1-84527-272-2

Cover design: Sion Ilar, Welsh Books Council

Published by Gwasg Carreg Gwalch,
12 Iard yr Orsaf, Llanrwst, Wales LL26 0EH
tel: 01492 642031
fax: 01492 641502
email: books@carreg-gwalch.com
internet: www.carreg-gwalch.com

This book is dedicated to

Rosemary Zöe Lodwick
18 May 1941 – 27 February 2010

We met because of jazz, and all our married life she was there to support me and the music. She provided a warm welcome for the musicians of the Harlem Blues and Jazz Band; she looked after my dear friend Dill Jones in his later years. She kept a beautiful garden; she was always ready to set the house up for television crews – including for a Penblwydd Hapus programme, when she knew six months before that Johnny Williams (Louis Armstrong's bass player) and the Harlem Blues and Jazz Band were flying over to take part in the programme! On that occasion she even – uniquely in our marriage – had to withhold the truth from me in order to make sure I didn't know about it!

She was my wife, my friend, my partner, and I miss her.

Contents

Foreword

by Dr Al Vollmer,
founder of the Harlem Blues and Jazz Band

There is something very special about jazz music. It originated in America and is a product of the Afro-American culture. Within a remarkably short time it spread to every corner of the globe and ignited the passions of generations of youths.

Elders generally, in all countries, decried the music as a corrupting influence on established morality. Some of the fiercest opprobrium emanated from the pulpit, as all religions are fearful of anything that might upset the status quo.

Even the Black church, which has contributed so powerfully to the mix, condemned jazz and blues as the Devil's Music. Be that as it may, thousands of youngsters experienced an epiphany from this music. The beauty, pulse, syncopation, harmony and freedom through improvisation of this music spoke directly to them, often in a manner that would seize them for life.

There were many avenues for participation. There was direct communication with jazz music by face to face contact, or indirectly by correspondence. American jazz fans would go and hear the musicians at the venues where they performed, while overseas devotees could catch the musicians when they travelled abroad.

A large number of enthusiasts started record collections and made heroic attempts to discern culturally, or by direct contact, the personnel behind each precious recording. British jazz researchers became conspicuously adept at compiling discographies after the French had led the way and perspicaciously acknowledged jazz music as a true American art form.

It is now a cliché that jazz is the sole American contribution to the arts. Academic institutions now provide jazz courses along with significant jazz archives both in the US and abroad. This was not the case, even in the 1940s when the young Welshman Wyn Lodwick discovered jazz.

Apart from these more sedentary or academic pursuits, the need to participate physically expressed itself through dance. There were many forms, but the Lindy Hop or the Jitterbug developed into the most popular and satisfying way of creatively interacting with music.

Finally, there were those who felt compelled to play this music as a means of expressing their profound captivation by this new idiom.

Jazz bands were formed with the music acting as a limitless avenue for personal and collective catharsis. This was, without question, the case with Wyn Lodwick.

Wyn caught the jazz bug when he was about thirteen years old. Fortunately for him, and for jazz, the prognosis was terminal. From the standpoint of chronology, Wyn belongs to the second generation of enthusiasts, i.e. those who came to the music around 1940, after many of the seminal, classic jazz masterpieces had been created and recorded – King Oliver's Creole Jazz Band (1922), Jelly Roll Morton's Red Hot Peppers (1926) and the Armstrong Hot 5s (1925–26) and the Armstrong Hot 7s (1927), prophetically the year of Wyn's birth.

Wyn's path to jazz followed a fairly common route. First of all he came from a musical family. Eldest brother Alwyn and only sister Margery both played piano while his younger brother Mervyn played both piano and vibes. It was only natural for Wyn to follow suit and with some background in piano, he took to the clarinet around 1940.

This was precisely the time - in fact, it was New Year's Eve 1939 – when he heard the tune 'In the Mood' on a radio broadcast. This led to the discovery of the swing bands that he heard featured on AF Network and the BBC.

The Welsh clarinettist Harry Parry had a sextet that played jazz on the BBC's *Radio Rhythm Club*. Parry also delivered talks and played historical jazz records every Thursday night from 6.30 to 7.00. This introduced Wyn to Fats Waller and Louis Armstrong. The latter's recording of 'West End Blues' (a King Oliver composition) and 'Knocking a Jug' came as a revelation, and from then on there was no turning back.

Philip Larkin, the late British author and jazz critic described this phenomenon in *All What Jazz: A Record Diary 1961–1971*. He, too, found the black jazz recordings of the 1920s and 30s all-pervasive.

He wrote: 'this was something we had found for ourselves, that wasn't taught at school … There was nothing odd about this. It was happening to boys all over Europe and America.'

In fact, a few years later, around 1944, a fifteen-year-old in a suburb of Stockholm, Sweden, was discovering jazz with equal fervour. That teenager was me. I, like Wyn, started with 'In the Mood', a tune composed by the black tenor saxophonist Joe Garland.

The coincidence of 'In the Mood' is perhaps not so startling because at his time an American film, *Sun Valley Serenade*, starring John Paine and Sonja Henie, the famous Norwegian figure skater, and featuring the immensely popular Glenn Miller Orchestra, was being shown in cinemas in many European countries. 'In the Mood', along with 'Chattanooga Choo Choo' and other Miller hits, was a prime feature of this film. The original Glenn Miller recording, with an arrangement by the black musical genius Eddie Durham, was unavailable due to the start in Europe of World War II. However, the British bandleader Joe Loss had recorded a carbon copy of the Miller recording and it was this version that excited the sensibilities of both Wyn Lodwick and myself.

If you believe in destiny, Wyn and I were bound to meet eventually because we both needed jazz to be an integral force in our lives. To cut a long story short, I emigrated to America, became an orthodontist in Larchmont, NY, and in 1973 formed The Harlem Blues and Jazz Band with King Oliver's trombonist/blues singer, Clyde Bernhardt.

Early on, the Welsh pianist Dill Jones, who had settled in New York City following his stint as ship's pianist aboard the *Queen Mary* ocean liner, became the pianist in the Harlem Blues and Jazz Band. Dill was the pianist on the band's first overseas tour to Scandinavia in 1976. He is also the pianist on one of the band's first recordings in the company of such significant jazz luminaries as Doc Cheetham, George James, Charlie Holmes, Tommy Benford and, of course, Clyde Bernhardt.

Wyn was by now an accomplished clarinettist, band leader and full-time school teacher. Significantly, he was also a friend and musical colleague of Dill Jones.

Dill and Wyn met in 1959 when Dill guested with Wyn's Celtic

Jazz Band at a yacht club ball. After that they appeared together and separately at many concerts and jazz events. Educationally, Wyn became a fully-fledged lecturer at a Further Education College and in 1966 became head where he, in conjunction with arts and culture departments, promoted jazz concerts. Dill appeared there in concerts and later Clyde Bernhardt guested with Wyn's Welsh Jazz Quartet.

When Wyn first visited America in 1973 he came to New York where he stayed with Dill who, at the time, lived in a small apartment on East 12th Street. Within months of retiring from teaching in 1981, Wyn began working on a new TV series on current affairs, where he performed with his band. He was now paying annual visits to New York, always linking up with The Harlem Blues and Jazz Band. He sat in on the band's steady gig at the Gingerman, an upscale restaurant at 64th Street and Broadway opposite Lincoln Center.

Thanks to efforts by our mutual English friend and jazz aficionado the late Peter Carr, Al Casey, Fats Waller's famous guitarist, had consented to come out of retirement and participate at the Gingerman engagement. Here he joined Bobby Williams, trumpet; Eddie Durham, trombone (he had been responsible for Glenn Miller's arrangement of 'In the Mood'); George James, alto sax, later replaced by Eddie Chamblee, tenor sax; Gene Rodgers, piano (famous for his piano intro on Coleman Hawkins' epoch-making recordings of 'Body and Soul'); Johnny Williams, string bass, and Tommy Benford, drums. Later, Wyn worked with a Welsh TV crew on a documentary on his annual visits to New York City.

Part of that documentary, *Five Roads to Harlem* (Five Roads being a village near his home in Wales) was filmed at the home I share with my wife Dot at 11 Dogwood Lane in Larchmont, NY. This spacious house with a wonderful view across Long Island Sound lent itself to large jazz parties, often with as many as a hundred people in attendance, most of them jazz musicians. Among them was Doc Cheetham. Louis Metcalf, Bill Dillard and 'Wild' Bill Davieson trumpet; J C Higginbotham, George Mathews, Snub Moseley, Clyde Bernhardt, Eddie Durham and John 'Shorty' Haughton, trombone; 'Happy' Cauldwell, Gene Mikell, George James, Charlie Frazier, Eddie Chamblee, George Kelly and 'Buddy' Tate, saxophone; Dill

Jones, Gene Rodgers, Charlie Bateman, George 'Ram' Ramirez, Charles 'Red' Richards and Norman Lester, piano; Al Casey, Lawrence Lucie and George Baker, guitar; Johnny Williams, All Hall, John 'Peck' Morrison and Jimmy Lewis, string bass; Tommy Benford, Cozy Cole, Benny Greer, Belton Evans, Johnny Blowers and Ronnie Cole, drums; Princess White Durrah, Miss Rhapsody, Laurel Watson, Helen Humes and Gwen Cleveland, vocals.

The various musicians would form different combinations, and Stanley 'Fess' Williams would compere and arrange the order of performances, often with Greely Walton, who had given up playing, looking on. Wyn would join in on these festivities and would, of course, have a blow on his clarinet, fitting in perfectly with these veteran jazz musicians.

Wyn's CD recording *My 50 Years in Jazz* on his own label (WL 003) gives full testimony to his prowess as a musician, clarinettist, band organiser and entertainer. He surrounds himself with stellar jazz musicians, giving ample space to them as well as to himself. The fresh treatment of each tune is paramount rather than an attempt to present a *tour de force* for the clarinet alone.

Wyn can get around his horn and plays with plenty of swing and imagination. He is skilled at shifting from register to register and his chalumeau playing is outstanding. Some of this is, perhaps, as the liner notes of his CD proclaim, that Wyn's blues style epitomizes the strong connection between Celtic 'hwyl' and African/American 'soul'. Wyn's Welsh/American connection, his great friend Dill Jones, certainly had the 'hwyl'.

Wyn also filmed in the 1990s when the Harlem Blues and Jazz Band had a six and a half year residency playing every Saturday night at the Louisiana Community Bar and Grill in downtown Broadway, between Bleeker and Houston Streets in New York City.

Other encounters occurred in Europe, Belgium in particular, because one of the band's sponsors, Renaat Savels, an artist and vocational arts teacher, engaged the band to perform in the school where he taught. Wyn, a long-time friend of Renaat's, would come across the Channel to join in on these occasions.

Wyn came over to Harlem for the funeral of Johnny Williams at the Lutheran Church on 145th Street. Johnny, one of the most recorded bassist in the classical jazz idiom died at the age of ninety, having graced the Harlem Blues and Jazz Band for twenty-eight years, the longest tenure of any member of this on-going band.

Perhaps the most memorable of Wyn's encounters with the band, which involved considerable secrecy and skullduggery, was the time when we turned up in Wales unannounced as a surprise on a televised programme for Wyn's sixty-fifth birthday party.

This foreword only scratches the surface of Wyn's many-faceted endeavours. In order not to steal any thunder from the ensuing pages, I wish to acknowledge our deep and lasting friendship and point out that Wyn has led a fascinating life and that he has worn many hats with distinction and honour.

To delve deeper into his many experiences and triumphs, I heartily recommend an attentive perusal of the story that follows.

Al Vollmer
January 2010

Chapter 1

Some view the past and relive it by looking through the eyes of memory. But I usually tend to listen to my past and relive it through the ears of bygone days. My memory is not primarily stirred by pictures but rather by the sounds and noises of the Llanelli that no longer exists. It was the Llanelli of my boyhood and my youth; Llanelli, 'the town that I have loved so well'.

The noises and sounds of the town would stir me from my morning slumber and lull me to sleep at night. Noises and sounds would shape my days. I would wake every morning to the clacking sounds of the steel workers' clogs hitting the pavement beneath my bedroom window, tip-tapping like ticking clocks. The shriek of the seven o'clock hooter would quicken the beats. Then, the one o'clock hooter would announce the dinner break, while the last hooter at five would proclaim 'down tools'.

Every morning at eight, the circular saw at Harry Bach's timber yard would moan like a giant in pain. Joining the shrill orchestra there would be the ships' hooters as they sailed in to the various docks: North Dock – four hoots; GWR Dock – three hoots; Neville Dock – two hoots; the Northumberland Dock – one hoot.

Against the trumpeting hooters as a counterpoint I would hear the clanking noise of shunting goods trains and the grumbling of the big crane. And then the rushing noise of coal pouring from the hoists like black Niagaras, as ships like the *Polmanter* and the *Kajak* emptied their bellies as they swayed at anchor.

From the Marshfield works I would hear the churning noise of the big wheel that worked the steel mill, and the whine of the metal sheets as they were rolled, pleated and sliced, sounding like the screaming of tortured trolls.

There were industries everywhere, all based on goods connected with steel. There was Batchelor Robinson's, Moorwood's, Thomas and Clement, the Bury works, the Old Lodge, the Waddle Foundry, Llanelli Steel, the Old Castle and the Stamping, where the saucepans that gave Llanelli its most distinctive icons were produced. All had their different sounds.

Then there would be the usual street noises. Neighbours would shout their greetings. Uncle Gwilym with his horse and cart would be selling coal. James the Fruit calling out the names of the wares in his cart. And Kelly the rag-and-bone man would blow his cornet to summon us out with our unwanted old clothes and scrap. He was known to all as Kelly Toot-Toot. GWR's stately Shire horses would ferry goods that had arrived on the train. And Harold the Oil with his tank wagon shouting, 'Lamp Oil! Lamp Oil!' This would bring out Mam with a small tin churn that Harold would fill from a tap below the tank. Mr Purvis the Milk would then arrive shouting 'Milk-o! Milk-o!' and Mam-gu's jug would be filled to the brim from a tap behind the milk-tank wagon. Jack y Bigyn would

Mam with Alwyn, Mervyn and me in Mam-gu's garden, about 1932

arrive with a load of bread in his chain-driven van. And then to me the sweetest sound of all, the tinkling of bells on the handlebars of ice cream vendors on their tricycles. All day the street would echo with a cacophony of industrial and street sounds, the clanking of cans, the ringing of bells, trams lurching by and the clip-clop of horses' hooves blending with the calls of the traders, all combining to create a warm and friendly symphony.

And the sounds of music. I cannot recall a world without music. Our house would echo with some form of music from morning till night. It would have to compete with the cracking sounds of the burning anthracite in the kitchen grate and the hissing of the gas lamps at night.   And there would be singing. Mam was a member of a local choir and would sing as she worked. Dad would forever be playing records on the gramophone; he also played the piano. And Uncle Ifor would be practising his clarinet at all hours.

Next door to Mam-gu's house, where we lived, old Mrs Powell would sing like a love-sick thrush. I can hear her now, her voice drilling through the party wall. Her favourite song was 'I Saw You in the Park'.

Me in Mam-gu's garden in the early 1930s

Mam, Elizabeth Mary Rees, came from Cydweli; Dad, Thomas John Lodwick, was a local man from Felin, or Felin Foel. He lost a leg in the Great War while fighting at Ypres. He was brought home to recover at Llanelli in Stebonheath. Both of them attended the same chapel and presumably that is how they met. Dad's father, John was also local. My Mam-gu on my father's side had died long before I was born. Dad had a brother, Wilfred, who had three children, Joyce, Gwyn and Howard. Dad's sister, Elizabeth, was married to Uncle Gwilym the coalman. She died young leaving two children, Dyfrig and Olwen.

Mam was a nurse who had worked at the munitions factory on the Burry estuary near Machynys. Some of the brass cylinders produced there to make shells adorned the mantelpiece. Therefore, though Mam and Dad probably knew each other previously, it was the war that brought them close. Had Mam not tended Dad following his accident they might not have married. I remember Mam tending to other people too. When Eddie Powell from next door fell and split his tongue, Mam stitched the cut with a needle and thread.

Mam was the only girl in a family of five children born to Charles Allen Rees and Mary Jane King. Mam's family, the James', lived in Gwendraeth Row near Cydweli Castle. They were the keepers of the castle keys. Tad-cu had come over from Blaenau Gwent to find work in the steel industry. They married and settled down in the one of the factory houses called the Forty, named after the forty houses built there.

Tad-cu was an excellent tap dancer. His forté was to dance on top of a barrel in the Myrtle pub on his way home from working at the Marshfield. My sister Margery inherited his gift, although she didn't dance on a barrel! I have often wondered whether it was from him that Alwyn, Mervyn and I inherited our sense of rhythm. Three of the four sons, Ifor, Bert and Charles were musical. Johnny was the odd man out. Uncle Charles, in particular was a fine tenor. Uncle Bert played the piccolo and the flute. And Uncle Ifor was a member of the Town Band and played the clarinet, the Jew's harp, and the ukulele banjo just like George Formby.

As well as playing these various instruments Uncle Ifor would also sing for us children before we went to sleep at night. One of my favourites was 'The Laughing Policeman'. I would love to hear him sing that one. But when he sang the old Negro song 'Poor Old Joe', I would cry:

> Gone are the days
> When my heart was young and gay,
> Gone are my friends
> From the cotton fields away,
> Gone from the earth
> To a better land I know.
> I hear their gentle voices calling,
> 'Poor old Joe'.
> I'm coming, I'm coming,
> For my head is bending low.
> I hear their gentle voices calling,
> 'Poor old Joe'.

Uncle Ifor kept around fifty canaries and every Sunday morning, having cleaned their cages, he would practice the clarinet. Then, in the afternoon, looking smart in his red jacket with brass buttons and black trousers, he would play with the Town Band on the bandstand at Parc Howard.

Even then I was fascinated with Uncle Ifor playing the clarinet. At home he would usually play marching music, songs like 'Goodbye Dolly Gray', a song from the Boer War. He would also play Welsh tunes such as 'Calon Lân'. He left me his clarinet in his will.

Uncle Ifor also owned a wonderful contraption known as the Polyphon, bought in Holland. It would play records, a kind of early juke box. It stood in the corner of the front room and stood taller than me. Its mechanism consisted of brass clockwork, and a penny in the slot would trigger it to play a selected record. The records,

*Dad with his little three-wheeler,
and Neil sitting in it*

huge plate-like brass discs measuring around a yard in diameter, were stacked inside and a series of pegs would correspond with a series of holes to play the tunes like a fairground hurdy-gurdy.

For a while Uncle Ifor trod the boards as one half of a comic double act with a man called Jack Simmonds. They were well suited, with Uncle Ifor small and Jack tall and thin. One night they were billed to play at Pontarddulais, but they lost one another and spent most of the night touring the pubs hoping to meet in time for the show. They must have looked quite a sight, Uncle Ifor blacked up and wearing a white suit and a turban and Jack dressed as a vicar. When they finally met, they were drunk as lords.

An important musical institution in the town was the Llanelli Symphony Orchestra that was based in Capel Als and led by Elfed Marks who played the violin. Elfed lived just across the road from us. He was a great influence on youth music in the area for many years. I also have a vague memory of the 1930 National Eisteddfod held on Parc y Dre when I was three years old. Mam was a member of the Eisteddfod Choir conducted by Edgar Thomas, Llwynhendy.

After he had recovered from his war wounds, Dad was given work at the local telephone exchange. Following their wedding he and Mam had moved into Mam-gu's house at 38 Marble Hall Road. To me this was the most important house in the world. It was there that I was born. It stood between Capel Als and the hospital.

The day I was born was apparently very stormy with the sky full of drifting snow. When Dad realised that Mam's time had come he sent Uncle Ifor to fetch Nurse Beynon from down the road. By the time she arrived, I had been born.

The year of my birth, 1927, was a very important year historically, as Uncle Ifor insisted on reminding me. J. G. Parry Thomas had been killed when his car Babs crashed on Pendine Sands as he chased the world land speed record. And Cardiff City, for the first time ever, brought the English FA Cup to Wales.

I was the second of four children. My big brother Alwyn had been born seven years earlier. Eighteen months following my birth, my younger brother Mervyn was born. Because of the short age gap between us we remained very close throughout the years. Then, in 1934 my young sister Margery was born.

Alwyn holding Margery, with me and Mervyn outside Mam-gu's house in 1937

My parents decided to name me John Allen Wynford Lodwick. My father was Thomas John and Allen came from Tad-cu, Mam's father. I have no idea where the Wynford came from. Then Mam realised that my initials would spell JAWL, the Welsh name for the Devil. The order was therefore changed to Wynford John Allen Lodwick.

Many have asked me where my surname originates. Well, Lodwick was originally a Flemish name, Lodevijk. They were a family of craftsmen specialising in silk-weaving. In the fifteenth century they were very much in favour with the Dutch royal family but then they were discriminated against and they fled to Wales because of persecution, around the time the Huguenots did something similar. They settled on half a dozen farms in Carmarthenshire. And some of us remain.

When I was only three the family moved to the Rhydyfelin area of Pontypridd, where Dad had been offered a new job with the Post Office telephone exchange. We settled at 7 Holly Street. Alwyn started school there but I was too young. We were like fish out of water there, the only family in the street that was Welsh-speaking. There was a smattering of Welsh among the older generation. But the neighbours couldn't believe that Welsh-speaking children like us existed.

I recall that Dad brought his old Columbia gramophone with him. He would play tunes by Peter Dawson, such as 'Sheep May Safely Graze' and 'In a Monastery Garden'. Other favourites were 'In a Persian Market' by Ketèlbey, and Thalben-Ball playing 'Parade of the Toy Soldiers' on the organ, as well as popular pieces by composers like Percy French and Irving Berlin.

One advantage of living at Pontypridd was that it made visiting Cardiff so much easier. I well remember the music pouring out of the record shops there when I was a child. I managed to memorise the notes of 'San Sebastian'. Visiting Cardiff became a great adventure to me.

But the family was unhappy living in Pontypridd. The longing to be back in Llanelli was only deepened every time Uncle Ifor called with his pockets full of sweets and his head full of stories of the old place. Then, after three years' exile Dad was offered a job back in Llanelli, again with the telephone exchange. I can remember the joy of being driven in a taxi from the station back past the Half Moon and Capel Als back to 38 Marble Hall Road. It was drizzling, and ever since that day, I have loved drizzly weather. Indeed, it is my nicest kind of weather.

We were reinstated in Mam-gu's home. It is a place firmly fixed in my memory. There was, of course, a parlour. There on the table lay the family Bible alongside the skeleton of a sunfish and an elephant's tusk. Parlours in those days were not for living in. They were places where you left jelly to set and where bodies were left to rest in open coffins till the day of the funeral.

Life mostly turned around the kitchen where Sunday night was the climax of the week. Tad-cu would sit in the corner sucking on his pipe while the room would be packed with relatives and friends on their way home from chapel. There they would talk of the sermon, the weather and the Scarlets' performance at Stradey the previous day.

I can see the room now. Hanging on the wall by the window was a print of 'The Thin Red Line' depicting the brave men of Rorke's Drift holding out with rifles against a horde of black savages armed with spears. Very British.

On the window sill in the kitchen would perch the radio built by Uncle Ifor. One of his great heroes was John Scott-Taggart, editor of the *The Wireless Constructor* magazine. Another hero was F. J. Camm, editor of *Wireless World* and *Practical Wireless*. These magazines would include blueprints for building radio sets, two-valvers, three-valvers and four-valvers.

In the December 1933 issue of *The Wireless Constructor*, Scott-Taggart published a detailed blueprint for building an ST400 radio. Uncle Ifor taught me to build my own set, a crystal set with attached headphones. I became acquainted with the various components that were central in building a radio set – the coil and the condenser. And I remember the words written across the coil in the form of a question, 'What are the wild waves saying?'

A long aerial ran from the back of the radio to a high pole on the roof of the shed. One day Dad was giving the shed roof a new covering of tar when he heard a snipping noise. He looked down and there was Gilbert Harries snipping the wires that anchored the pole to the shed. Gilbert was a rough diamond. Indeed, he had once managed to escape from Norwich Prison. Dad allowed him to continue for a while but then, suddenly, he reached down and painted Gilbert's face with tar. He never returned.

Thanks to Uncle Ifor's radio I was able to listen to the world heavyweight championship fight between Joe Louis and Tommy Farr from the Yankee Stadium, New York in 1937. I was sound asleep when Uncle Ifor woke me and carried me quietly downstairs on his back to the kitchen to listen to the epic encounter.

But even more important, it was over Uncle Ifor's radios that I was first able to listen to music played by the big bands of Ambrose, Henry Hall, Harry Roy, Maurice Winnick and Geraldo. There were bits of radios everywhere. Little did I realise at the time that all this would prepare me for a career involving radios in the Navy and later in centres of education. But one thing intrigued me. I noticed that the window curtains were slowly turning yellow, and then to brown. And they began turning brittle before rotting from the bottom up. It was only later that I realised that it was the effect of the acid from the batteries feeding Uncle Ifor's radio. Mam-gu was losing her curtains inch by inch.

The great turning point of my life, however, was when Dad bought a piano from Nield's music shop for 68 guineas, which was a lot of money back then. It was a Bell overstrung piano with an iron frame. Dad was only earning around two pounds a week so it was quite a sacrifice. My eldest brother Alwyn took to it immediately. And he began calling in Nield's shop to buy sheet music. He would then play them on the piano, popular pieces of the day like 'My Prayer', 'Deep Purple', 'Scatterbrain' and 'Harlem', as well as more classical pieces such as Mozart's sonatas.

Another important piece of furniture was the bookcase. I would climb up to rifle through the books. I once fell down and broke my wrist. But this never put me off.

Reading to us was a priority, especially reading the newspapers. To a confirmed Socialist family the *Daily Herald* was a must. Mam's family were Liberal, but Dad managed to win her over to Labour. I remember on election days a car with a red sticker on its windscreen stopping outside the house to pick up Mam and Dad and drive them to vote up the Bigyn.

I can remember Communists making inroads in Llanelli at that time. We had a primary school teacher nicknamed Dai Pep. I remember him making speeches from the Town Hall steps on behalf of the Communist Party. Another teacher, this time at secondary school, Lloyd Humphreys, campaigned on behalf of the Communists. He had come down to Llanelli from Blaenau Ffestiniog.

As well as the *Daily Herald* we would take all the weekly papers, the *Star*, the *Mercury*, the *Dispatch* and the *Guardian*. But Sunday was the big day for newspapers. We would buy the *Sunday Dispatch*, the *Graphic*, the *Pictorial*, the *News of the World*, the *Empire News* and the *People*. In addition we bought magazines such as *John Bull* and *Tit Bits*. And there were comics, of course, the *Dandy* and the *Beano*, *Jingles* and *Film Fun*, the *Funny Wonder* and *Modern Wonder*. And later, as I got older I would buy *Wizard*, *Hotspur* and *Champion*.

Sunday was an important day for a very different reason. It would turn around the chapel, Zion Welsh Baptist Chapel near the Stepney Hotel. As children and young people we would attend Sunday School and the children's service, where T. R. Jones would give us illustrated talks. Such meetings would be held in the vestry, but then we would all join the adults at the chapel to listen to that great preacher, Jubilee Young, who was our minister. He was there throughout my childhood and during my youth, when I was baptised.

I can still see Jubilee clearly in his tail coat with his mop of thick dark hair. In the pulpit he would survey us over the heads of the deacons, T. R. Jones, Mr Williams and Mr Walters. Mr Walters had experienced a religious conversion when he was at sea. Also there was Twm Amen, so nicknamed because of his habit of Amening everything Jubilee spoke from the pulpit. To us children, Jubilee was God. But he was not an angry God. He was the God of love, a man that was easy to approach, and one that always spoke to us in a kindly manner.

Some 800 worshippers would attend every Sunday. And Zion was only one of many chapels in the town. The other Welsh chapels, New Chapel and Capel Als would also be full where hymns would flow like waves breaking on the shore. On the way to Zion for the six o clock meeting we would pass the Salvation Army Band on its way to their location in the town centre. Then, in chapel Jubilee would greet us with his fine voice and then he would present the first hymn. It seemed to me the whole town was singing.

I have always loved hymns. As a child I would sing 'Rwy'n canu fel cana'r aderyn' *(I sing like the bird sings)* and 'Hoff yw'r Iesu o blant bychain' *(Jesus loves little children)*. Even then I loved some of the more adult hymns like 'Diadem'. Its stately sounds created a picture of a battleship fighting huge waves.

Around half past six, Jubilee would begin his sermon. He would not finish until five minutes past seven when he would reach the 'hwyl'. Preachers like him were the pop stars of their era. He would begin slowly in a low key and gradually build up a head of steam until he reached a kind of chanting peroration. Then, suddenly he would come to an abrupt stop. That was his style. He was a great actor as well as a great preacher. And naturally there would be a moral at the end.

The chapel had its own choir and the organist was Sid Lewis. I would often stay behind to listen to Sid playing as the congregation filed out. I loved stately tunes like 'Finlandia'. Listening to Sid was an emotional experience that would often reduce me to tears.

In charge of Sunday School was David Emlyn Morris, who worked for the GWR. He would be in charge of collecting the annual Sunday School trip contributions. The choice every year was Porthcawl or Tenby and we would travel by train. Mam and Mam-gu would accompany us children. On that day we would be allowed to wear sandals. Down to the Wern we would go to catch the train. After it had pulled in, Mr Morris would open the carriage doors and ensure that we were all on board.

At Porthcawl there would be a huge fair on Coney Beach. I would immediately head for the motor boats. I was already being attracted by boats. I would steer my boat around a small island. At Tenby we would first of all fill our bellies with fish and chips before heading for the beach. Whichever happened to be our destination – Porthcawl or Tenby – Jubilee would be there with us.

An important event on the calendar was the Singing Festival or the 'Gymanfa Ganu' every Easter Monday. The Market Hall would be jam-packed, with all the area's chapels contributing. The children's festival was held in the morning and the main festival in the evening. The hall would be a cauldron of song and of light.

In addition to the trip there would be our annual holidays when we would stay in a holiday camp at Pendine. The Council ran the camp, and as Uncle Ifor was a Council employee we were sure of a place. There were rows of wooden huts near the beach, but we slept in a large bell tent. I can still smell the methylated spirits used to light the stove. Along the beach racing cars would roar, but we would find a safe place where we would play cricket. We travelled there by bus – but one year Alwyn decided to cycle there and back. On his way home it started to rain. It turned into a rainstorm and by the time he reached Carmarthen he was soaked to the skin. The only answer was for him to stay overnight at the James' house at Cydweli.

On another occasion we went to Aberystwyth, where the whole family stayed with a Mrs Richards at 30 South Road. This was close to the harbour so I was in my element. Alwyn was old enough to plan his own activities. Mervyn was ill and was confined to his bed. So Dad, on the sly, took me along to the railway station. There we caught the Cambrian Coast train through Aberdyfi and to Porthmadog from where we caught a bus to Llanberis and the travelled on the narrow gauge line to the summit of Snowdon. I remember that the price of the all-inclusive ticket, which was valid for a week, was thirty shillings. I also remember wearing an Ovaltinies badge in my lapel. When we returned and Mervyn heard of our trip he was livid. Strangely, when he celebrated his seventieth birthday, the surprise present his daughters Catherine and Bethan bought for him was a visit to the summit of Snowdon!

One aspect of the Llanelli of my childhood has stayed in my memory over all the years, and that was the light that shone on the town every night. On Saturday nights especially I would peer over the garden wall and see lights everywhere, street lights, neon lights above the shops and pubs. And the coloured lights of the cinemas. There were six cinemas in Llanelli then, the Odeon, Vintz

Mervyn, Dad and Mam, and Margery, Aberdyfi beach, around 1938

Palace, the Hippodrome, the Regal, the Llanelli Cinema, and the Dock Cinema.

The cinemas were instrumental in bringing American music to Llanelli. There would be long queues snaking along the streets outside, and as a child I felt that I knew James Cagney and George Raft, Marlene Dietrich and Myrna Loy as well as I knew the people who lived in our street. Then there were the cowboy actors, among them Ken Maynard, Roy Rogers and Buck Jones. Many of the supporting films were serialised, with every episode ending when our hero was in mortal danger, clinging with his fingertips from a cliff or tied to the railroad as a train came thundering onwards. For a whole week we would be kept on tenterhooks not knowing his fate. He would, of course, always make it through.

The music of some of the films was all-important. It was at local cinemas that I first saw famous bands like the Glenn Miller Orchestra and the Dorsey brothers for the first time. Previously I had only heard them on Uncle Ifor's radio. Now I could see what they looked like.

Dad first took me to the pictures. And on one occasion he was given free admission because he himself was appearing on Pathé News. Members and ex-members of the Welsh Guards were honoured by the king on St David's Day and Dad was among them. Because of his handicap he was personally greeted by the king and

Mervyn, Dad, Margery and Neil in the 1950s

was presented, like the others, with a leek. What an honour for Dad! A leek for a leg! And being allowed into the cinema for nothing!

On Saturdays at the Regal there were matinees for kids. Seats cost two pence and five pence each. Only children of the 'crachach' sat in the five-pennies. The place would be teeming. The commissionaire was an officious man referred to as Carnera, named after the famous Italian heavyweight boxer of the time. And we would provoke him by rolling empty pop bottles down the aisle. Here again there was music – before the show, during the films and at the end. Just before war broke out I remember a German oompah band playing in the town centre. Many local suspected them of being German spies. Maybe they were.

Llanelli was already a cosmopolitan town with many incomers having moved in to find work at the steelworks and in the docks. Ships sailed in carrying cargoes of pit props for the coal mines in the Gwendraeth Valley and would sail out carrying cargoes of steel and coal. Italians had settled and had opened cafés specialising in frothy coffee and ice creams. Across the street near Zion Chapel was Sartori's. Perigo had opened a café in Stepney Street. Another prominent Italian family in the town were the Antoniazzis.

The Italians would cycle round the town on their trikes with refrigerated boxes on the front. There would be locals making ice cream as well. Eiddwen's shop sold lovely ices, as did Cooper's shop. But the Italians were regarded as the experts in this field of confectionery.

The arrival of mains electricity was a big day for the town. Previously we had paraffin lamps with wicks and mantles. There were also hissing gas lights. Mam-gu would always have a lamp burning behind the front door that would be lit every night. And on various tables in the kitchen and the front room, lamps would sit on various tables. I can still smell the burning paraffin.

I associate the hissing of the gas lamps with Christmases of old. They contributed to the cosy atmosphere. On Christmas Eve we would hang our stockings on the rail above the fireplace. Early the following morning, the house reeking of roast turkey and Dad and Uncle Ifor's cigars, we would empty our stockings of fruit and nuts. And invariably included would be a bar of 'Five Boys' chocolate. Made by Fry's, these bars would be covered in wrappers bearing five pictures of a boy showing various emotions ranging from Desperation, showing him crying and on through Pacification, Expectation, Acclamation and ending with the beaming face of Realisation.

At Christmas time, Mam's family from Cydweli would call, Uncle James and Aunti Greta. Their son, Terry – who was to become the famous musician Dr Terry James – would also call with them. I remember Terry when he was only around seven years old standing on a chair and going through the motions of conducting us in singing the anthem 'Man's Days are Like Grass'. Even then he was suggesting how big a talent he would become.

The back kitchen was the heart of the house. It was there that the gas stove stood. On what we would describe as Fudge Day, Uncle Ifor would send us down to Jenkins' shop to buy sugar, a tin of Tate and Lyle's syrup, a tin of Nestlé's condensed milk and a pinch of vanilla. The syrup tin always carried a picture of a dead lion with bees settling on it and the slogan 'Out of the strong came forth sweetness'. All the ingredients would be boiled in a saucepan and then poured onto a tray to cool and set.

Presiding over everything from the settee would be Tad-cu, Mam's father, pulling on his pipe. Behind the settee would be Uncle Ifor's Boosey and Hawkes clarinet in its black wooden case. Tad-cu would always talk to us in English. Above him on the wall hung a calendar with a moveable red square on a transparent strip that could be moved from date to date. And as the square neared 25 December the excitement would grow from day to day.

I would always look forward to Thursdays when Mam-gu would bake us a meat pie. It would be full of diced beef and sliced potatoes, and an egg cup would support the crust. I have never since had a tastier meat pie.

Above the stove was a trapdoor leading to the loft. There, having climbed a stepladder, we would find ourselves in an Aladdin's Cave of delight. The greatest treasure of all up there was an old wind-up gramophone with an attached horn to relay the sound, exactly like the one in the His Master's Voice advert, only without the dog.

The back garden was an important area. It was there that Uncle Ifor grew his tomatoes and where Mam kept chickens. It would be a great day when a batch of day-old chicks arrived in a box from the station. Invariably there would be one little chick too weak to follow the rest. Dad would then wrap it in the special sock he used to cover the stump where his leg had been and place it in front of the fire to recover.

The garden was enclosed by a low wall built by Uncle Ifor from clinkers fetched by us from the iron work tips. Uncle Ifor would dress the clinkers and cement them in place. There are still many such gardens in Llanelli with walls made from the waste of the old works.

No garden would be without its shed. In our shed was a carpenter's bench with tools of all sorts for both wood and metalwork. This interest was, no doubt, part of the people's inheritance. Craftsmen at the iron and steelworks would tend to bring their work home with them. It was in Tad-cu's shed that I learned wood and metalworking skills, rather than in school. Even when I was only seven years old I could fashion small wooden chairs. I could identify the various timber, black beech, cherry and sapele and so on.

I learned craftwork, like everything else, from Uncle Ifor. I delighted in wood and metalworking. I would be constantly surrounded with Meccano parts. I even built my own bike from spare parts.

Nothing would surprise us children. When Uncle Ifor brought home a monkey from India, it was no surprise. Both he and Uncle Bert had been to India. Taffy the monkey was like one of the family. He would even eat Sunday lunch with us. One day Taffy escaped and ran up the back lane to Marged Isaac's garden. Marged was famous for her ginger beer. Every Saturday night we would call at her house to buy bottles to drink with our Sunday lunch. When Taffy arrived, Marged was busy sieving coal round the back. Taffy leapt on her back, frightening the life out of her.

We never owned a dog but we did have a cat called Blackie. I remember Blackie well. Uncle Ifor and I would play football on the table top with a ball made from compressed paper. He taught Blackie to play in goal. When we flicked the paper ball, Blackie would leap like an acrobat to stop us from scoring.

And referring to a cat brings me to a traumatic experience. The memory can be very selective at times. Take that English FA Cup final of 1938. It isn't the fact that George Mutch scored the winning and the only goal from the penalty spot in the last minute that makes me recall that day. It was rather the fact that Uncle Ifor, just as the winning goal was scored drowned six kittens in an old oil drum that he used to water his tomatoes at the far end of the garden.

But my memory is now leaping too far ahead. Before Tad-cu died there were eight of us living at 38 Marble Hall Road. After he died I remember seeing the invoice from the undertaker lying on the kitchen table. The funeral had cost £28. In 1933 we were given our own house up the street in number 78, opposite the Grammar School. But I decided to stay on at Mam-gu's house with her and Uncle Ifor.

Margery was born in the new house. Two apprentice nurses, both from Pontrhydfendigaid, were working at Llanelli Hospital and lived at 78 with our family, so Mam had no problems with the birth. Despite the fact that I actually lived at number 38, I would spend a lot of my time at number 78, and I well remember the swishing sound of the nurses' starched clothes as they walked up and down the stairs.

Mam and Margery in the garden of 78 Marble Hall Road in the 1940s

The time arrived for me to start school and I well remember my first day in Stebonheath Infants School. I wore a yellow shirt. I started in Miss Aubrey's class, which was the Welsh-speakers' class. She attended our chapel, Zion. The English-speaking children, although they were Welsh, went to Miss Adams' class. Language apartheid started early in Llanelli.

In class we all had our own slate for writing on. Today it's all done on computers. One of the attractions of school was the percussion band. While Miss Aubrey played the piano we would march around the sports hall playing our instruments. I played the tambourine. Others played simple trumpets or would beat on drums or hit triangles.

Before long I was seven and was moved up from the infants to the primary school, Ysgol y Parc. The Welsh medium school, Ysgol Dewi Sant, had not yet opened, but its future head, Olwen Williams, was one of our neighbours. She also ran meetings of the Urdd Aelwyd, part of the Urdd Gobaith Cymru (*Welsh League of Youth*) that I joined.

Miss Bowen was my first teacher. She had a shrill voice. She played the piano and played it out of tune. Even at seven years old I could recognise that. Her piano playing grated on my ears so much that I was glad to move to Standard Two where Miss Harry, who did not speak Welsh, was the teacher.

One of the teachers was a man we called Howells Bach, the devil incarnate. He would fix his beady little eyes on us while the cane trembled threateningly in his hand all day. He would teach us to write by copying sentences from the blackboard on to bits of card cut from placards he collected from the newspaper shop. The sentences, naturally, would be in English, meaningless sentences such as 'The quick brown fox jumped over the lazy dog'.

Around this time, when I was in Standard Four, a diphtheria

epidemic hit the town. And I caught the infection from, of all people, Uncle Ifor. He was the Council's Hygiene Inspector, working out of offices that stood by the Mansel Hotel, where the Verandah tandoori restaurant stands today. Unknown to himself he was a carrier of the infection, having been in contact with sufferers. He realised that I exhibited all the symptoms of the nasal type of diphtheria and decided to keep me home from school. I remember jumping up and down on the bed in a temper and even swearing. I never usually swore. At least, not when Mam could hear me. I was then taken to the infections centre.

I quickly recovered but a boy who shared a desk with me, a lovely lad called Hubert Harris, caught the infection and died. I can see him now, a quiet boy wearing a green blazer. I still feel guilty for being responsible for passing on the infection that cost him his life.

By Standard Five things got better. The teacher, Mr Thomas was a nice man who liked music. Every day, morning and afternoon we were taught to sing. He gave us the lot, harmony, different voices – I would sing alto – and singing from the Modulator. A Curwen's Modulator, naturally. Learning sol-fa was like discovering a new language as I learnt to develop the ear. Indeed, it was not only a listening experience, I was taught to see music. This proved to be all important to me in later life. I was able to learn all the voices, tenor, bass and even alto by ear. And the end product, of course, was to master harmony.

In addition to the music lessons we were able to listen to music programmes on the BBC's *Radio Relay*. We would be supplied with pamphlets accompanying the programmes. Unfortunately it was all in English. One song I still remember was 'Dashing Away with the Smoothing Iron'. Another was 'Here's a health unto His Majesty, with a fa-la-la, fa-la-la-la'. And 'Jerusalem', of course, in which Jesus' feet never trod on Wales' green and pleasant land. Jesus was English. The Empire and the Royal Family were omnipotent. I remember in 1935 we all received metal mugs to celebrate King George V's Jubilee. Two years later we received Coronation mugs.

It wasn't as if our home was different to any other. Supplements in the *Chronicle* and the *Herald* carried stories and pictures of the Royal Family. And at school, that language apartheid still continued. We would be divided into groups. It was a case of 'Welsh Boys, go to

Mr Thomas' and 'English Boys, go to Mr Reed.' And later on the English Boys would naturally chose French rather than Welsh.

One activity that crossed language boundaries was rugby. This was the glorious era of the great Albert Jenkins. And we would crowd onto Stradey Park to wonder at him and Stan Williams and Ifor Jones, as well as other local heroes. These, during the week, were ordinary workers. But come Saturday afternoon, they became superhuman.

I remember Stan one Saturday morning, with an important match to be played that afternoon, facing a load of bricks left near the station. Stan worked for the Council and had to load the bricks on a lorry before he could leave for Stradey Park.

Albert, however, was the star. He liked his tipple, but that would never have an adverse effect on his playing. Later, the Albert Jenkins Society was formed as a tribute to him. The instigators were men like Cenwyn Edwards and Elis Owen, who later became important figures in Welsh television. The members would meet prior to a cup match and I often played at these meetings. And if Ray Gravell was present he would be sure to sing a song or two. There was only one rule for members of the Albert Jenkins Society. No Swansea Jacks were allowed in.

When I was a lad, Stradey Park would be packed to the rafters. And when we played Swansea it seemed there were more policemen there than there were supporters. There would be enmity, and this would often escalate into fisticuffs. But of course there would also be a band playing and a lot of singing.

As a family we also loved soccer and often went to Stebonheath. I remember an influx of players from Scotland to Llanelli, players like McNab and McAllister and later, of course, the great Jock Stein when Llanelli climbed to the Southern League. I can still reel off the names of the opposing teams, Blaengwynfi and Treharris, Troedyrhiw and Tongwynlais, Ton Pentre and Penrhiwceiber and Merthyr. Stebo was also a boxing venue, and I remember watching fighters like Ronnie James and Larry Gains boxing there.

However, the family game was cricket. Alwyn, Mervyn and I played regularly. And whenever we visited Mam's family at Cydweli, Terry James would join us for a knockabout near the Mason's Hotel. Up Heol Dŵr, in a house named Arosfa, lived Auntie Liz and her brothers, Uncle Ivor and Uncle Bob. It was Auntie Liz that encouraged Terry to play the piano.

In addition to the usual sports we would also play games such as 'Cat and Dog', involving hitting a short piece of wood tapered at both ends with a stick, making it jump high in the air. The trick then was to hit the piece of wood again before it landed on the pavement. All kinds of games were based on washers and wheels, reflecting some of the town's industries. Then there was 'Ticker', a version of 'Hopscotch' with grids marked on the pavement with either chalk or a lump of coal. 'Knock-and-run', or in Welsh, 'Cnoc-a-whiw', was another popular, if naughty, pastime. We would tie a length of string to a door-knocker and pull at the string from a safe distance. The poor neighbour would answer the knock only to find there was no-one there.

No-one enjoyed a happier boyhood. But as the old saying goes, all good things come to an end. When he was fifty years old, Uncle Ifor decided to get married. This led to my banishment from Mam-gu's house. And for a while the music died.

Chapter 2

When Uncle Ifor wed Auntie Maggie at the end of the Thirties, I was told that, in future, I would have to live with Mam and Dad and my brothers and sister in the new house in number 78. Overnight, the magic and the fantasy disappeared from Mam-gu's house. I then realised how Adam felt when he was expelled from the Garden of Eden.

The miraculous Polyphone was exiled to the shed. The clarinet now lay in its box like a cold corpse in its black coffin. Uncle Ifor did buy a second-hand organ and one Saturday, when Auntie Maggie was out shopping, I called to see the instrument. I was even allowed to play it. But that was the first and the last time I was allowed to do so. When Auntie Maggie arrived home from the shops the organ joined the Polyphone in the shed. Number 38 Marble Hall Road was now a silent mausoleum, a house devoid of music.

However, there was some good news. Coinciding with my exile from number 38, I discovered that I had passed my '11 Plus'. Around this time, Dad would take us on mystery trips on summer evenings. And we were due to go on one the evening that my results came though. We called in Mrs Williams' paper shop in Heol Als and discovered the results in one of the local papers. This made the trip even more exciting.

On our mystery trips we would travel on various buses leaving from outside the Town Hall. The bus companies included Sage, Pudner, James, and South Wales Transport. James would also run a bus to Aberystwyth. It was known as the Radio Bus for the simple reason that it had a radio installed, and during the journeys we were able to listen to various broadcasts.

Naturally, on mystery trips we would not be told of our destinations in advance. From the Town Hall we would leave for Llandovery, Llangadog, the Black Mountain or Cuckoo's Corner and we would always stop for chips on the way home. On the night that the exam results arrived I recall that I won the raffle held among the passengers. The first prize was a whole salmon. I even remember the winning number. It was number four.

There was no shortage of friends when I was a child. Many of our relatives themselves had children and they would all call every Sunday. Mam's family had children. There was Aneira, Uncle Johnny's daughter, who was particularly close. Then there was Denys, Uncle Bert's son. Outside the family there was David Griffiths from up the road. Then there were Ieuan Thomas and Hugh Davies. We would gather on the back lane to play cricket. Even back then, David was quite the entrepreneur. He would concoct a liniment he called Bruise Oil to rub on bruises caused by the impact of the hard cricket ball on our bodies. This he would sell for a penny a bottle.

We would sometimes pitch tents at the back where we would organise evening feasts. We were known as the Hospital Gang or the Marble Hallers. Sometimes another gang from down the docks would come up to challenge us. How we feared the leader of that gang, Donny Lewis. We were influenced by the various Western films we would watch at the cinemas. We were the cowboys and the Docks Gang would be the Indians. Donny Lewis even dressed like a Red Indian. One morning when I went out to the garden I found an arrow sticking out of the shed door with a piece of paper wrapped around it. Written on the paper were the cryptic words, 'We have taken your sticks!'

When the chimney was swept we would gather the soot and stuff it into empty tins and use them as soot bombs. Upon arriving home we had to be scrubbed clean and all our clothes washed. Often Edna, Aneira's elder sister, would help Mam with the washing. She would also enjoy being there when Mam read the tea leaves for the neighbours. Mam fancied herself as a fortune teller.

Success in the 11 Plus meant that I moved on from Park Street School to Llanelli Grammar School. I started in Form 2R. I soon realised that here there was less music there than at Park Street School, where we would be taught music daily. But now I was given the opportunity to learn Music as a real subject. There was a school orchestra, and the morning assembly was an integral part of the morning activities. There, Ronnie Cass would play the piano as we filed out to our lessons. He would play modern pieces like 'Tuxedo Junction' and I would hang around till the very end to listen to him. This meant that I was often late for my lessons. But my good friend Hamilton Davies, or Hammy, who was in charge of the attendance register, would always mark me as being present.

Hammy and I had been childhood friends. But we quarrelled over football. He kicked my new leather football high in the air and it landed on a spike on the park fence and burst. This was a special ball, a real T-Panel football bought from the Market Street sports shop for six shillings and sixpence. We, the Marble Hall Gang had an official soccer fund. We would do all kinds of chores to raise money. I ran messages for Miss Samuel the Shop on Friday evenings and on Saturdays and all the bob-a-job money would go to the fund. Hammy and I were soon back on friendly terms. Our mutual love of music ensured that.

By now Mervyn and my cousin Terry had started buying cheap Eclipse records at Woolworths. They sold at six pence each. My favourites at the time were 'Old Faithful' by Gene Autrey, 'Play To Me', Gypsy' by Henry Hall, 'Gilbert the Filbert' by Basil Hallam and 'The Wheel of the Wagon is Broken' by The Sons of the Pioneers. Among the Sons of the Pioneers was Roy Rogers, appearing as Leonard Slye. Terry's favourite was 'Wagon Wheels' by Paul Whiteman.

During my second year at grammar school, war broke out. Morning assemblies became sad occasions as we listened to the headmaster, T. V. Shaw, reading the list of names of killed or missing ex-pupils, perhaps a member of a missing plane crew shot down over Germany, dead or captured. All were young. It seemed as if not a day would pass without someone being named. At school we had our own five-seater de Havilland Rapide, a DC2. The school had its own branch of the Air Training Corps, and we would be allowed to dismantle its engine and rebuild it. It seemed that all school life revolved around the war. There was also a branch of the Army and RAF Cadets, but no Sea Cadets group, although there was one based in the town.

The area had already witnessed an interest in planes just before the war when Sir Alan Cobham came to nearby Gorseinon with his autogiro, the forerunner of the helicopter. Cobham would provide flying trips and Uncle Ifor and Uncle Bert would often attend the air show. To them it was a great adventure.

I well remember the arrival of the evacuees. Two were taken in by Uncle Ifor and Auntie Maggie. They were Terry Joys and Sylvia Day from Balham in London. Sometimes, when the English teacher, Mr Thomas – or Dreamy to us – taught some of the London girls we would push messages written on scraps of papers to them through holes in the partition.

The greatest change brought by the advent of war to Llanelli was the extinguishing of the lights, both literally and figuratively. Where once I could see the town from the back garden ablaze with lights, there was now darkness. The lights above the shops and the cinemas, the neon lights and the street lights all went out. The future also seemed dark. The same was true everywhere. As Sir Edward Grey announced at the beginning of the Great War, 'The lights are going out all over Europe, and I doubt we will see them go on again in our lifetime.' Or so it seemed.

Another great change was the situation in the mills and factories. Under the emergency bill, women joined the men on the factory floor to produce war necessities, especially munitions.

Now, of course there was a limit on food bought in the shops. Every family was tied to its ration book. Coupons were at a premium. Whereas before, Mam could buy a pound of butter in the market, she was now limited to a few ounces. And tinned salmon became a luxury that would use up a week's allocation of coupons. This was the era that heralded the appearance of margarine. I hated the stuff, but there was no choice.

On the positive side, Mervyn and I began taking piano lessons. My great hero in those days was Teddy Wilson. He had performed with Louis Armstrong, Benny Goodman and Billie Holiday, and we had heard him over the radio. And this was when I first encountered swing, with tunes like 'Southern Fried', 'Missouri Scrambler' and 'Biting the Dust' offering me a new dimension over the airwaves.

Locally, bands like the Denza Dance Orchestra and the Ritz Orchestra, The Ambassadors and the Mayfair Dance Orchestra were formed. They all had exotic names. Among the leading local musicians was bass player Hubert Hughes, who would later join my band. Many of the instrumentalists were members of the Llanelli Town Band, the Llanelli Silver Band or the Elfed Marks Orchestra. Mervyn and I were too young to be allowed to attend the dance halls so we listened outside.

At the Odeon, Henry Hall's Guest Night would occasionally be staged. One night in 1940 it was broadcast live on radio and I still remember Jack Bonser on the clarinet, Freddy 'Curley' Mann on the trumpet and vocalists Jack Plant and Betty Driver. She, incidentally plays the part of Betty Turpin on Coronation Street. That night the orchestra played one of Harry Parry's compositions, 'Parry Opus' and the tune 'Eccentric'. Little did I realise at the time how important a part Parry would play in my life.

One of the best-loved voices of the war was, of course, Vera Lynn, known as the 'Forces Sweetheart', with her songs of hope such as 'We'll Meet Again' and 'The White Cliffs of Dover'. Another was Anne Shelton, the 'Forces Favourite', with 'I'll be Seeing You' and 'A Nightingale Sang in Berkley Square'. She appeared with Geraldo, Bing Crosby and Glenn Miller. A favourite song of the times was 'Keep the Home Fires Burning', composed by Ivor Novello during the Great War and revived. Gracie Fields also played her part in raising people's spirits during those dark years. But casting his evil shadow over the airwaves was the mocking voice of Lord Haw Haw and his eerie greeting, 'Germany calling, Germany calling'. His voice would send shivers down my spine.

At the beginning of the war we were all allocated our personal family air raid shelters. These Anderson Shelters were built, or rather buried in back gardens. They were made of corrugated iron with a half-domed roof, where various emergency tools and implements were kept in case the shelter needed to be occupied overnight. During the excavation for its foundation, various pieces of Llanelli pottery were unearthed. Today, Llanelli pottery is rare and very valuable.

When war was declared, Dad took it upon himself to give us children some bayonet practice. He used a rail from the fender and rammed it time and again into the shed door. He remembered his training with the Guards. And today the wheel has made a complete turn. I now have a nephew who is a member of the Welsh Guards and has been on two tours of Afghanistan.

To us in Llanelli, war became a fact of our daily life. The Luftwaffe carried out continuous bombing raids on Swansea, especially the Docks. They were the biggest westerly docks in Britain with miles of railway sidings. Another target was Neath, an important fuel distribution depot. Ivor Emanuel's family home at Pontrydyfen was hit. Ivor, who was only three years old, was pulled out of the rubble in the garden but he lost members of his family.

One raid on Swansea in February 1941 lasted three days. By 1943 the town – now a city – had suffered forty-four bombing raids. During some of these bombing raids Mam would take us up to the top of the road near the hospital. From our vantage point we would be able to see the reddening sky as the Heinkels emptied their fuselages. First there would come the incendiaries, lighting up the docks like candles on a birthday cake. Then the bombs would drop.

There were welcome diversions. I would often visit Swansea, especially the Empire on a Saturday where bands like Joe Loss and his Orchestra would perform. Maurice Winnick would also perform in *The Dorchester Follies*. Winnick described his music as 'the sweetest this side of heaven'. I would normally go with Hamilton Davies, and we would commit to memory the names of every musician that appeared. Other kids would collect names of famous soccer players.

A few bombs landed on Llanelli, especially around the North Dock, where there was a fuel depot. Indeed, a bomb once landed on someone's piano in his front room. At Pembrey there was a munitions factory and there the works canteen was hit. We had heard the Heinkel all morning, its droning engine creating terror amongst us. Many were killed. On my way home from school I saw a lorry pass by ferrying fourteen of those injured to the hospital.

By now Alwyn, my eldest brother was working in Bristol, another city that suffered a great deal of bombing. Naturally, we all worried over his safety. He worked in

My brother Alwyn in his youth on a visit to Rhosygwalia, Y Bala

39

a factory that manufactured gyroscopes for aeroplanes. He also did similar work at Stroud later on.

He then volunteered to join the RAF. This again was worrying. We had already lost a cousin, Arthur, who was also in the RAF. He was blown to bits in his plane. Alwyn experienced some terrible events. When the Lancasters returned there would often be casualties. And it was the rear gunner, known as 'Tail-end Charlie', who was most vulnerable. On average these crews would only last seven days before being either injured or killed. Alwyn would often have to hose down the blood from the rear cabin after the dead or injured gunner had been carried out.

He served a part of his service out in Lahore in India, where he spent three years. One night he had a very narrow escape. He was walking back to the camp in the dark when an approaching car full of officers from the mess lit up the road in front of him. There, in the glare of the headlamps he saw a coiled cobra preparing to strike him.

When Alwyn worked in Stroud I was very jealous of him. On Sunday nights he would frequent band concerts in the Gloucester area where bands like Oscar Rabin and Joe Loss performed. He once sent me Joe Loss' autograph jotted down on the back of a cigarette packet.

At that time I would regularly visit the YMCA where I played snooker and table tennis. But at 6.30 every Thursday evening everything stopped. It would be *Rhythm Club* time on the radio.

The programme would be introduced by Harry Parry. He was a clarinettist from Caellepa, Bakery Lane, Bangor, and he became my mentor. Indeed, he became my greatest hero. Harry, unlike most bandleaders of the time, played swing. On *Rhythm Club* he would also present items on the history of jazz.

I decided to find myself a clarinet tutor. I had been left Uncle Ifor's clarinet and I now wanted to become a serious instrumentalist. I found an ex-soldier, Jack Price, who had been invalided during the Dunkirk campaign. He played with a local band. I started playing the Albert System clarinet but then changed to the Boehme fingering system.

It was Harry Parry's influence that determined I should play jazz rather than dance music. I felt dance music was too sober, too formal. To me, jazz was different. It was exciting. And because I was one of the only instrumentalists in Llanelli playing jazz at that time, I felt rebellious. Naturally, at formal dances I was still prepared to conform. I had no choice. It was, after all a job of work.

Like Alwyn earlier, I began frequenting Nield's music shop. And I began spending my pocket money on records by Sidney Bechet and, of course, Harry Parry, the former on Brunswick Black Label and the latter on the Parlophone Blue Label. I would then play them on Dad's gramophone.

Dad worked nights, from eight in the evening till eight in the morning. I couldn't play the gramophone or the piano while he slept. There I was with a new record burning in my hand. How I yearned to play it, to hear it for the very first time! But no, Dad was sleeping. The only solution was to place it on the turntable, switch on and place the nail of my first finger in the groove instead of the needle. I even grew my nail long for a clearer sound. Thus I could listen to the tune without disturbing anyone.

Sometimes Alwyn would risk playing the piano while Dad was asleep. He would play in a low tone, and rather than switch on the light he would use his bicycle lamp to illuminate the copy. On New Year's Eve 1941 I heard Joe Loss playing 'In the Mood' on the radio for the very first time. He later adopted it as his signature tune. I hummed the tune in Alwyn's ear and he immediately played it back to me.

I was now buying the *Melody Maker* every week, paying three pence for it. Because of the war and the emergency powers there was a shortage of paper so it was only a four-page broadsheet. It listed where and when all the bands played, from Glasgow down to Swansea. My immediate task, however, was to discover where and when Harry Parry was appearing.

Because of the war and the constant danger of bombs, various homes near the school were designated as places where pupils from further away could shelter. Whenever there was danger, even in the middle of an exam, the pupils would be moved out at a minute's notice and taken to these homes. Designated for our house were two pupils, one of them being Glyn Howells. Glyn, who was lame and wore callipers, was a brilliant boogie-woogie pianist. After chapel on Sunday both of us would call at Sartori's Café to drink frothy coffee, share a secret cigarette and play the piano in the back room.

At this time I appeared with a band on stage for the first time. It was with Paul Vincent and his Rhythm Boys. His name was Vincent Arthur. But his real name was too bland. The letter 'V' was prominently displayed on every music stand on stage signifying not only Vincent but also Victory.

This, to all intents and purposes, was Llanelli's very first jazz band. And for the first time, those attending came to listen as well as to dance. We were all schoolboys. Glyn was on piano, Idris Williams on trombone, Denzil Adams on fiddle, Vincent on drums or fiddle and I was on clarinet. We would play in all the small local venues.

We made our first appearance at the Oddfellows near the Thomas Arms. We then played at St Barnabus, at St Peter's and other venues. Then we graduated to the Astoria down near the station. The owners were the singer Dorothy Squires from Pontyberem and her partner Billy Reid. She became a world star and Billy was a very successful musician and composer. Three of his songs reached number one in the American charts, 'Tree in the Meadow', sung by Margaret Whiting, Eddie Fisher's version of 'I'm Walking Behind You' and 'The Gypsy' by the Ink Spots. Dorothy later married Roger Moore.

The occasion was the railway workers' annual Good Friday concert in 1941. It was the first time I ever stood in the blue spotlight on stage. It was a great feeling. I well remember taking up the clarinet solo in Woody Herman's classic, 'The Woodchoppers' Ball'.

On another occasion we made an appearance on the radio programme Workers' Playtime during the lunch hour at the Morris Motors factory canteen in Felinfoel in 1942. I was now approaching the end of my school days and my life was dominated on two fronts, jazz and the war. Jazz was now flowing throughout Europe and spreading worldwide. In France, for instance, Django Reinhardt and Stéphane Grappelli's music was popular. But my scrapbooks included not only pictures and stories of jazz giants. They also included pictures and stories of dogfights between British planes and the Luftwaffe, with Spitfires and ME109s vying for superiority in the skies above.

Cricket was our delight. Alwyn played in the Lancashire League. Mervyn captained the Llanelli cricket team. My most unforgettable cricketing event was on a day in August 1968 when I went to St

As a member of the Llanelli hockey team, 1953

Helen's in Swansea to watch Glamorgan play the West Indies. I was about to enter through the turnstiles when a cricket ball almost decapitated me. Yes, I had arrived just when Gary Sobers hit his first six of six off Malcolm Nash's fateful over.

Unlike my two brothers I never shone in cricket. But I did serve as captain of the Llanelli hockey team. My son Neil, however, kept the sporting tradition alive by not only captaining the borough cricket team but captaining the Llanelli Wanderers rugby team as well.

The closest the war ever came to us as a family was on a day in May 1941. Mervyn and I were playing cricket on the Flat Field on Pen-y-fan. We were disturbed by the sound of an approaching plane. We knew from its coughing and spluttering that something was wrong. Then we spotted a Hawker Hurricane flying low towards us. It seemed as if it was returning from the south of England over Swansea towards Pembrey and obviously it was in trouble. Mervyn had been about to bowl and the plane was heading straight for us. It passed so close that I could see the oil dripping onto the pitch. It was obvious that the pilot had intended crash-landing and we could see the damage to its fuselage. The pilot pulled up and just cleared us and headed for the Stradey cricket ground. The plane touched the overhead electric cables before landing further on at Pwll where the cricket ground is today. There, with very little land to spare he

43

*Waclaw Wilczewski, the
Hurricane pilot who saved the lives
of Mervyn and me on Pen y Fan*

deliberately hit the ground short just behind Isfryn and Bethlehem Chapel. He could have landed safely on Pen-y-fan but rather than risk hitting Mervyn and me he placed his own life in danger by choosing a far more dangerous landing place.

When the Air Warden arrived at the scene he saw the pilot kicking the plane in frustration. He was swearing in a strange tongue, leading the Warden to suspect the pilot was German. Just a year later he was killed when his Spitfire was shot down by a German fighter during a dogfight. Years later a local historian discovered that he was a twenty-year-old Polish pilot, Waclaw Wilczewski, of the 316 Polish Squadron based at RAF Wessex.

That year, 1941, was to be a fateful year for a different reason. In August of that same year, there happened an event that was to change forever my approach to jazz. That's when a large crew of American soldiers arrived at Llanelli. They had sailed over on the USS Uganda, dodging U-boats and the Luftwaffe on their voyage to Swansea Docks. They were billeted in Llanelli, the white GIs based in the Drill Hall in Murray Street and the black soldiers in wooden huts at Furnace.

They came to Llanelli, as they came to other areas of the UK, to prepare for the coming Normandy landings. Their arrival coincided with my appearances in my first band and when I began attending dances and musical events. I remember seeing American soldiers in Burton Hall at Neath when Harry Parry played there. And I remember Harry announcing, on behalf of the US Military Police: 'Will all the coloured troops please leave now at ten o'clock. The white troops should remain for half an hour.'

Problems would often arise leading to clashes between white and black US soldiers. I remember seeing a black soldier being thrown out of a lorry outside the Town Hall having been stabbed by white soldiers. I had no inkling at the time of the apartheid existing in America. To me, America was what I saw in films, where there were no racial tensions. It was only later that I realised that the situation in some southern states was as bad as, if not worse than, that in South Africa.

The situation was vividly evident in a fair held near Moriah Chapel. Incidentally, Harry Parry's music had become so popular that it was played over the loudspeakers at the fair. But I was surprised to discover that there existed a policy of banning blacks from the fair on one night and then banning white soldiers on the following night. They were not allowed to mix.

But the arrival of the American soldiers opened a new door to me. Many were musicians. I would talk to them of Count Basie and Cab Calloway. One night, two of the black musicians called at Nield's music shop bringing their instruments with them. They later performed with us in an upstairs room at the shop. I heard later that both were killed on Sword Beach during the Normandy Landings.

Having made friends with American soldiers we were invited as a band to perform for them at a dance they organised at Carmarthen. They were billeted where Glangwili Hospital stands today. There was a collection of Nissen huts there and the camp was a GI hospital. We were due to play on a Sunday night. Earlier in the afternoon I had just arrived home from Sunday School when a six-wheeler US Army lorry pulled up outside the house. The GIs had a vehicle centre near Caersalem Chapel. I heard a knock on the door. Mam answered the door and I saw two black GIs standing there. This wasn't strange at all. Almost all the drivers were black. And I heard one of them ask, 'Does Wyn Lodwick live here?' Mam, as she did with everyone who called, invited them in for a cup of tea. They gladly accepted. Even though she had never spoken to a black person before, she saw nothing strange in inviting two black men into the house. To Mam, bless her, the only thing she recognised as being black was coal.

The other members of the band arrived one by one and we travelled up to Glangwili in the back of the lorry. At Glangwili we performed our spot. I believe they were quite surprised to hear a Welsh jazz band playing tunes that were popular back home in America, tunes such as 'The Woodchoppers Ball' and 'Doggin Around'. On 'Doggin Around', recorded by Count Basie, blind saxophonist Elwyn Davies played a solo on his tenor sax.

Afterwards we were invited to the camp canteen where we ate with the soldiers. And we ate our food off a tray. Everything came on a tray with every item of food individually packed in containers, the meat in one, the potatoes in another and the sweet in yet another.

One Sunday evening in chapel I witnessed a strange episode. Two black GIs walked in to worship amongst us. They were probably attracted by the sign above the door announcing that this was Zion Baptist Chapel. And of course, many of the black GIs were Southern Baptist. Although the service was wholly in Welsh, they remained throughout. And when the sacrament was served one of the deacons, Mr Walters whispered something in the Rev. Jubilee Young's ear. He was obviously unsure of what he should do. Should the black visitors receive bread and wine? Jubilee Young nodded his head. And yes, they received the holy sacrament like everyone else.

The American GIs all left their various camps throughout the UK overnight to embark on Operation Neptune at sea and Operation Overlord on land on D-Day on 6 June 1944. A total of 1,465 died on the Normandy beaches, from Utah Beach to Omaha Beach. Some 5,138 were either wounded, went missing or were captured. Coincidentally my present drummer, Arthur Perry, transported some of those soldiers across the channel in a flat-bottomed boat.

Margery and Mervyn in Mam and Dad's garden

By June 1943 I had left school. I was sixteen. I found work as a wages clerk at Llanelli Steel's sheet metal section. I knew that this would only be a temporary job as my ambition was to go to sea. Next door to the office was located the ambulance centre where I would spend hours listening to Morse code messages.

At the time Harry Parry was appearing in Manchester in the British Dance Bands Final Round competition. Having made up a story that a relative was seriously ill I caught the train to Manchester and arrived home in the early hours of the morning and then went back to work, having missed a day.

Mervyn and I had discovered Johnny Hodges, an alto sax player who had performed with Duke Ellington. We had heard mention of him from Harry Parry on the radio. He had just recorded the tune 'Daydream' on HMV, and Mervyn and I had treated ourselves to a copy over Christmas. Our record collection was rapidly growing and becoming more specialised from week to week. Naturally, they were classical jazz records. Like any young man I was interested in girls, but not as much as my interest in jazz. As youngsters we would lounge on street corners watching what was referred to as the Monkey Parade. This involved the local girls walking around hoping to be accosted by the man of their dreams. Should he not appear, they would then look to one of us until the right man came along. But now we had strong competition from young men in uniform, especially the well turned-out American soldiers. By now the town was full of soldiers, some home on leave and others, like the Yanks, based there. The Monkey Parade route led along Stepney Street, round the York Hotel over to Boots and back round the block to Stepney Street.

The brothers in their uniforms: me in the Navy, Alwyn in the Air Force, and Mervyn in the Army

Following my stint as a clerk I decided to enter the Merchant Navy's South Wales Radio Training College at Caswell Bay. The centre had already suffered some damage caused by enemy bombing. I travelled daily by train to Swansea and on by bus. The course involved receiving and recording genuine messages from various ships. I managed to pass the examination and now it was a matter of waiting for placement on a ship I could join as a crew member. Meanwhile my official call-up papers arrived ordering me to join one of the armed services. I chose the Royal Navy. But before doing so I took the opportunity to visit Bletchley Park near Milton Keynes, where the revolutionary Enigma device for deciphering the enemy's secret codes was developed. I was accepted there but decided to turn down the opportunity of working there as a member of the Army. I decided instead to wait for the call to join my first ship. That call came in May 1944.

Before I could join my first ship I was summoned to the radio college at Aberdeen. But I caught vaccine fever and had to be treated in hospital. After I was released I was sent to pursue a course on radio at Walthamstow Technical College in London, a department

Me with a group of students in Walthamstow Technical College in 1945

attached to South West Essex College. This was a time when the English capital was a nightly target by the German V1 rockets known as Buzz-bombs or Doodle-bugs. It was a terrifying experience to hear them fly above the clouds. Even more terrifying was the silence when their engines cut out. That was the signal for those below that the bombs were about to land. And they could land virtually anywhere. I was staying in digs in the home of two sisters, Doris and Edith Flack. I would leave for college in the morning, passing ruins of buildings that had stood solid the previous night.

But through it all the music continued. I remember one night visiting the Assembly Halls where

Freddie Mirfield and his Garbagemen were appearing. They played on stage dressed like bin men surrounded with rubbish bins. They were a traditional jazz band and their clarinettist was Johnny Dankworth, who was embarking on what would prove to be a brilliant jazz career.

Following the completion of the course I travelled up to Scotland to HMS Scotia to serve as a petty officer working on transmitters. Then I travelled down to Petersfield to the Royal Naval Signals School to serve as a tutor. I was one of dozens of young people from Llanelli to join up, of course. Other members of the Paul Vincent and his Rhythm Men band had also received their call-up papers and we broke up. I was sent to Skegness, to the former Butlin's holiday camp. For the first week there was absolutely nothing to do. Then an officious sergeant handed me a knife and ordered me to cut the grass around the huts. What a situation! The war was at its peak, Hitler was knocking at the door and there I was cutting grass with a bread-knife!

Then one day I was sitting at the piano in the Toc-H Club when a stranger joined me. He introduced himself as Jim Frost from Southampton. I happened to be playing 'Royal Garden Blues' by Clarence and Spencer Williams, a tune popularised by Bix Beiderbecke. He was, he said, a clarinettist. We immediately became friends and we remain friends after all these years. Unfortunately, though, we were separated. He was appointed Education Officer as Midshipman and I was sent to Scotland to serve as a radio engineer with the rank of petty officer. There another door opened for me. I was now able to listen to The Voice of America, a radio station that promoted jazz.

One day I was summoned over the loudspeaker to call in the Divisional Office. There I was informed that I was to join what I understood to be HMS Craille. I had never heard of Craille so I had no idea of its location. Someone explained that it was a naval base somewhere on the Scottish coast. Then I realised that I had misheard the message. I was to join not HMS Craille, but rather *HMS Creole*. I soon learnt it was a brand new warship built by John Samuel White at Cowes. And what a coincidence. The Creoles live near New Orleans, the cradle of jazz. They are a mixture of Africans and French with their own brand of music. Duke Ellington composed a tune he named 'Creole Love Call'. There was no escaping jazz.

The Creole, *the ship I spent my naval service on*

Initially five of us joined the ship anchored in the estuary of the Medina river in Cowes on the Isle of Wight. My responsibility as telegraphy petty officer was to supervise those installing the radio system for the ship's maiden voyage. Together with the radar officer I was billeted in number 82 Mill Hill Road in Cowes.

The rest of the crew gradually arrived, including the First Lieutenant and then the Captain, Grenville Cowley, making up a contingent of 120 crew. Socially, times were good. We had our own cricket and soccer teams. And occasionally I would cross over to Southampton to visit Jim Frost. At his home we would play jazz records. I also appeared on stage with his band. We even made a record together of the great spiritual classic, 'Just a Closer Walk With Thee', one of America's greatest hymns. One of our favourite bands at that time was Bob Crosby and the Bobcats. He was, of course, Bing Crosby's brother and his signature tune was 'Summertime', composed by George Gershwin and included in his musical, *Porgy and Bess*.

After all the equipment had been installed on the *Creole* we went out to conduct tilt and speed tests reaching 36 knots. It carried four five-inch guns that turned on their axis, two up front and two astern.

We also carried anti-aircraft guns and six torpedo tubes. In addition we carried depth charges.

As a crew we were now members of the Portsmouth Harbour Authority. I was delighted when I heard that Mervyn, who had signed up with the Army, had been sent to Portsmouth Barracks. He visited the ship one day and the galley crew stuffed him with food. He couldn't believe the standard of cuisine we enjoyed compared to what he had to eat in the barracks. When he arrived he had just called in a music shop to buy one of Louis Armstrong's records.

In my uniform during my naval service

As I was in charge of the ship's sound system I would often play jazz records so that the whole crew could hear. And I naturally played Louis' record. I remember that it was 'Static Strut', with 'Muggles' on the flip side. It was on Black Label Parlophone. The ship's theme song, incidentally, was 'On the Sunny Side of the Street' by Tommy Dorsey.

Such was our love for music that we smuggled aboard a piano. We anchored it to one of the guns and covered it with the gun's awning. Unfortunately, one stormy day the piano was washed overboard and it sank.

Having completed successfully all its tests the *Creole* set sail for Derry in Northern Ireland, where we would be based. There we joined the Sixth Destroyer Escort Flotilla. On the way over we passed the Lizard and sailed up the Irish Sea past Pembroke. Looking longingly at the Welsh coast I was tempted to jump overboard and swim home. We soon arrived in Derry, on the Irish Republic border.

Our flotilla included the *Crispin*, which matched the *Creole* exactly, and four frigates, the *Loch Trallaig*, the *Loch Arkaig*, the *Loch Vayati* and the *Loch Fada*, as well as a number of submarines. We were the second in the group, behind the *Crispin*. Included in our duties was the use of ASDICs, involving sending a series of pulsing

With some of the crew and Gun No 3 on the deck of the Creole *1946*

sounds into the deep. The pulses returned with sounds indicating the presence of U-Boats. Should the sounds prove positive we would fire depth charges overboard. Usually, however, the only casualties were fish blown up by the charges. Hundreds would lie on the surface. We would collect some of them in nets and the staple diet on board for the next few days would be fish.

Numerous wrecks lay on the sea floor, the ships having been sunk by either the British or the Germans. Mallin Head in particular was a very dangerous shipping area where German subs often stalked. Among those sunk in the area was the *Llandovery Castle*, a hospital ship. Attacking a hospital ship was classed as a war crime of the very worst kind. The German captain attempted to obliterate all evidence by sinking all the lifeboats bearing the survivors. However, one boat managed to escape and the two dozen survivors lived to tell the tale. Almost 250 crew, medical staff and hospitalised passengers were killed.

When VE Day dawned on 7 May 1945 I was home on leave in Llanelli. That night, in my naval uniform I joined the hundreds of revellers that filled the streets. I was standing on a teeming Town Hall Square enjoying the singing and the cheering and the fireworks. Unfortunately a stray firecracker struck me in the eye injuring me and burning a hole in my coat. I was blinded in one eye for a month. What irony! I had managed to survive Hitler's V1 rockets in London but there I was, blinded by a firework in Llanelli while celebrating the end of hostilities in Europe! With a patch over one eye I resembled that other sailor, Nelson. I received treatment at Llanelli Hospital by a Doctor Phillipe, who just happened to be a violinist with the Berlin Philharmonic Orchestra.

Gradually the German warships and U-Boats yielded to the allies and many sailed in to Derry Harbour to surrender. I saw a film of some U-Boat Commanders yielding to their British counterparts and offering a hand of friendship. But to my disgust, some of those British officers spurned the offer. To me that was a great disappointment. Despite the odd exception, most of the German officers had fought honourably. Then, on 15 August the war against Japan ended. It was all over.

The VE celebrations continued for days and nights and the lights came back on all over Llanelli and over the whole of Europe. The smell of freedom filled the air. One of the most popular band tunes of the time had been written back in the twenties by Jack Yellen and Milton Alger. It was now so appropriate:

> Happy days are here again,
> The skies above are clear again,
> Let's sing a song of cheer again,
> Happy days are here again.

When I joined the Navy I signed on for the duration of the war, or HO – Hostilities Only. But I completed my allotted minimum period of three and a half years. I signed off at Christmas 1948. I received a glowing testimonial from Captain Grenville Cowley. Indeed, I was offered an extension to my service agreement. But I had been away from Llanelli and from Wales for too long. And home I went unsure of what my future held. Llanelli may have been re-illuminated, but my future aspirations were dark.

Chapter 3

After the euphoria of the cessation of the war had faded and I had left the Navy, I was totally lost and bewildered without any plans for the future, indeed without any discernable future. Rebuilding was now the priority. Rebuilding bombed houses and factories. Rebuilding towns and cities. Rebuilding communal spirit. Rebuilding confidence. But I found it very difficult to make a new beginning.

Alwyn and Mervyn, as well as Margery, had turned to teaching. They lost little time in finding their feet. They managed to make the transition to normality without any difficulty. But after three and a half years on board ship, where we had all worked as a team and were dependent on co-operation, I was cast adrift with no direction.

I had seriously considered extending my agreement with the Navy. But my roots were in Llanelli. Ideally I would have liked to continue my studies in radio technique and technology, but there were no suitable courses offered in the various training colleges. The only other field I could turn to was arts and crafts. I could train to be a teacher in that field. And that's what I reluctantly did. I had very little choice. That was the only alternative. I entered Carmarthen Training College.

Training and further education colleges were full of people like me, ex-service personnel trying to pick up the pieces. Fortunately, grants were available. Before the end of the war, those seeking training were almost exclusively young people, school leavers who went straight to college with very little experience of real life. Older students such as me, who were more mature and had served in the armed services, were more prepared to challenge authority. We would not suffer fools gladly. For instance, if we felt the food was not good enough we would make sure that the authorities were told and that they would do something to rectify the situation. If we were unhappy with the attitude of a lecturer, we would bring it to the attention of the authorities. We were not afraid to stand up for our rights.

During my first year at Trinity College Carmarthen I shared a room in one of the college's halls of residence. On my second year I lived in digs at Allt-y-cnap in Johnstown. I undertook a two-year course for prospective teachers following a higher course in art and Welsh.

In the meantime I married and my son Neil was born in 1949. Pat, my wife, was from Ystalyfera where she worked in a bank. Unfortunately things started to go wrong quite early on in our marriage. She was ambitious and moved to work as a financial officer for an open cast mining company. Her work took her away regularly on various courses and conferences. She had her mind set on moving to America. And this is what she ultimately did when Neil was still a

My son Neil in Mam's garden

young child. She left and we never saw her again. I do not blame anyone. These things happen in life, even though you may fool yourself into thinking they will never happen to you.

I was now back in the real world, a single father to a young boy. The Navy had sheltered me for three and a half years. It had been an artificial way of life to a large extent. But now I was a citizen of the world. But at least I was blessed with a family, and our family had always been close.

I also swallowed a large dose of cynicism. In the Navy, ratings had risen in rank on merit. And they were respected for what they had achieved. Life on the outside in the rat race was so different. Some lecturers at college had prospered as a result of either back-stabbing or toadying to those in authority. I sorely missed the close brotherhood of men that had existed in the Navy.

A kind of hierarchy existed in Llanelli at that time. I also found it true in Glamorgan. If you wanted to get on in the world there were four golden calves you had to worship. You had to be a Labour Party supporter, be a member of the Freemasons, be a prominent Scarlets adherent and be a Baptist. Should you qualify for all four, you were made. But if you were a Plaid Cymru supporter you had no chance. I did support the Scarlets and still had an affinity with Zion Chapel. But otherwise I was an outcast. And anyway, I have always been a Welsh nationalist.

Despite all this I managed to find a teaching job. My first post was as a teacher in Laugharne. The end of the war had seen the rise of Higher Education Centres in Carmarthenshire. An Englishman, Mr Cameron, from Newcastle, was in overall charge of the Laugharne Centre. The school headmaster, though, was Doug Bradshaw, a strict disciplinarian who would liberally use the cane. Yet he could be a very friendly character. I was totally against corporal punishment. I never once resorted to using the cane.

I lived in digs in Rosetta House near the Manse. Laugharne was known as an insular and introverted town. Unless you were born there, you would not be accepted. I knew some who had lived there for twenty years yet were still regarded as strangers.

The centre included a workshop for working in both metal and wood. There was a smithy, lathes and drills, and a science laboratory. Everything was brand new. The pupils and students varied in age from eleven to fifteen.

Numerous colourful characters lived in Laugharne. There was, for instance, a man known as Buddah. He lived in Ferry House next to the Boat House and was a deaf-mute. He was suspected and arrested for the brutal death of a local old lady, Lizzie Thomas, but he obviously was not guilty and was released. The murder happened in January 1953 after I left. Many locals suspected Ronald Harris of the murder, especially after he was hanged for the murder of his uncle and aunt, John and Phoebe Harris, later the same year. I would often see Ronnie driving around in his Land Rover. He had a bad reputation even then, and no-one risked crossing him. Little did I realise at the time that I would, years later, play the part of his father in an S4C production as part of a series on Dyfed murderers.

The predominant family in Laugharne was the Williams family. Billy ran the bus service there as well as the electricity service. His brother Ebbie owned Brown's Hotel. Billy was a great eccentric who always wore a big-game-hunter type hat. At his garage he had installed an engine taken from a German U-boat from the Great War and had adapted it as an electric generator that supplied the town. The system was rather primitive. When it rained, flashes would shoot out like blue lightning from the cables in the street.

Billy's brother Ebbie ran the Post Office as well as Brown's Hotel. Indeed, you could claim that the Williams' ran the whole town. I ran an adult course as night classes and every time I turned on the lathe, all the street lights would be extinguished. The Electricity Board then took over and paid Billy to install the wiring. He was paid a shilling and sixpence for every plug socket installed on their behalf. Billy made sure that every room in every house had a socket in every available spot. Billy and Ebbie were fine folk.

Once, in March 1951, Doug Bradshaw organised a trip in one of Billy's buses to Ynys Angharad Park, Pontypridd, so that a crew of us could see Tommy Farr fighting a boxer called Frank Bell. Tommy had retired for ten years before attempting a comeback. He had since won two fights. But this time in Pontypridd he was knocked out by Bell in the second round.

Often Mr Cameron and I would stroll around the town. One evening we turned off the main street to follow the lane above the sea. As we passed a house called Sea View I heard two people arguing loudly and heard a smash. Then a gin bottle broke at my feet. We had witnessed an argument between Dylan Thomas and his wife Caitlin. Fortunately, Caitlin's badly-aimed gin bottle had missed Dylan but had sailed through the window and just happened to miss us as well. At that time I didn't know them but I would often see them drinking at Brown's Hotel and holding court with the regulars.

The local policeman at Laugharne at the time was an ex-neighbour of mine, Dai 'Farmer' Jones. He had been in digs in Marble Hall Road in Llanelli. He was a very good boxer. Brown's wasn't renowned for closing on time and one night Dai raided the pub and took the names of all those drinking after hours. Among them were Dylan and Caitlin.

After laying the foundations educationally at Laugharne I moved to Trelech to attempt to tackle the same task there in a similar centre. I was still married

Me in the 1950s

then, and living in Ystalyfera, but was living in digs during the week at Trelech. I did attempt travelling daily by bus. This meant travelling on a total of six different buses. I had to leave at 4.30 in the morning and change buses at Pontardawe from Neath to Gwaun Cae Gurwen. There I had to catch the miners' bus from Ammanford to Carmarthen. There I had to wait for the Pioneer bus for St Clears where I then met one of the teachers, Miss Lewis, who taught Domestic Science at Trelech and she would give me a lift.

Once more I was given a brand new craft centre with all the latest equipment and tools. I found the Trelech people to be completely different to those at Laugharne. For one thing they all spoke Welsh while the Laugharnies were almost monoglot English-speakers. In fact, Laugharne wasn't even Welsh in character. Neither was it English in character. It was totally different to any other place.

The headmaster was Tom Williams. He was a lovely man. One of my contributions to the village was to lay a new cricket pitch and persuade the local authority to adopt it. I even staged a cricket match between the local team and Laugharne. Never have I seen two such different teams playing each other. It was difficult to believe that they lived in the same country, not to mention the same county. Yet, for some strange reason there was a great camaraderie between the two teams. They became friends on the cricket ground and, need I say, in the pub after the game.

I stayed for a while at Pant-y-berth farm. I enjoyed living there even though farming was totally alien to me. I was offered rented accommodation in the village, but Pat did not fancy living in the country. This was one of the differences that drove us further apart.

Then when Pat left I was forced to find work closer to Mam, as she was now looking after Neil. I was offered a post at Pontyberem. But in 1953 I was given the opportunity to take a course on mechanics and furniture design at Loughborough College. I thought the course would prove to be a valuable addition to my earlier training course.

I often performed in the Loughborough area. One of the many venues I played at was Quorn Hall, in the heart of hunting country. Many crachach lived in the area. And it was during my time at Loughborough that I enjoyed my greatest moment: I met Louis Armstrong. Louis and his All-Stars were on tour and were booked to appear seven miles down the road at Leicester's Granby Halls. With me were Gareth Griffiths and Dai Hayward, who were fellow students at Loughborough. Both of them went on to represent Wales in rugby. We travelled to the concert in a Railton, a huge American gangster-type car that wouldn't have looked out of place in downtown

Neil in Mam's garden

Chicago. It was coloured a metallic blue and Dai was driving. It was heavy on fuel, doing around nine miles to a gallon.

The hall was packed and we sat at the back. I decided, as I usually did before a concert, to have a little stroll around. I managed to reach backstage and I headed for the dressing rooms. I had often done this at the Empire at Swansea. I enjoyed nothing more than chatting to the various musicians who were appearing there. I knocked rather timidly on a dressing room door. Out came Louis' clarinettist, Edmond Hall. He had played with Teddy Wilson and had previously played with Louis at Carnegie Hall in New York. He was very friendly and we talked of jazz, of his technique in particular.

Then the vocalist, Thelma Middleton, joined us. She and Louis had immortalised the duet 'Baby, It's Cold Outside'. She joined the conversation and Ed Hall pointed out to me Louis' dressing room. I knocked on the door, but rather than hearing Louis' voice I heard a cadenza on the trumpet, Pa-pa-pa-da-pa-pa-da-pa. I took the greeting to be Louis' way of welcoming callers and in I went. And there in front of me stood the man himself with those big round eyes and the gleaming white teeth and the trumpet in his hand. There he was, the greatest jazz man in the world smiling at a Llanelli boy who idolised him. What a privilege!

'Sorry to impose myself on you, Louis', I mumbled.

Louis answered in that hoarse voice of his, 'Welcome, man'.

I then took the opportunity to question him about the show. Would he be playing songs of the Hot Five and the Hot Seven? He assured me he would, adding, 'I sure ain't goin' to play all that modern stuff. That ain't jazz, man. To me that's ju-jitsu'. Louis was part of the classical jazz tradition, just as Chopin and Brahms were in their particular field of music.

The highlight of the evening came when Louis signed his book. I had brought along a copy. I passed the book to him as well as my brand new fountain pen. He grabbed the pen in his fist and pressed it so hard on the title page that the nib almost snapped. I didn't care. A broken fountain pen was a small price to pay for the autograph of the world's king of jazz. I returned to my seat, my head swimming. The lads didn't believe me when I told them I had just been talking to Louis. They did when I showed them the autograph. And I still treasure that book.

Louis' story is a classic rags to riches tale. He was raised by one of his aunts and spent his childhood on the streets of Upper Town, New Orleans. He was continually in and out of correction homes for boys, where he was once sent for firing a gun in public as a New Year's Eve celebration. It was at the home that he was taught to play the cornet. He soon joined the home's band when he was thirteen years old. Even then he was a heavy cannabis user, a habit he never gave up until his death.

When he was eventually released from the home he was found a job hauling coal before he joined Kid Ory's Band and eventually King Oliver's Band. Oliver was his great hero. The rest is history, with Louis going on to form his Hot Five, his Hot Seven and his All Stars.

Louis specialised in scat singing, a form of singing without using recognised words. It was a kind of 'shooby-doo-ba-ba-di-ba' and so on. But part of Louis' greatness was his respect for all forms and styles. He performed with such diverse musicians as August Strindberg and Johnny Cash.

That night in Leicester was not my last connection with Louis. Later on I met Joe Muranyi, who joined Louis' All Stars as a clarinettist in the Fifties. I even bought one of his clarinets. Joe was a

Hungarian who played with many leading bands during the Fifties and Sixties. Previously I had stuck to Uncle Ifor's clarinet. His, however, was an Albert-style instrument and by then I had changed to the Bohème style. Back then a good second-hand clarinet would cost around £100. I bought another clarinet, this time from Bob Wilber, who was connected with the famous Cotton Club in Harlem. It became infamous during Prohibition. Bob was a former member of Sidney Bechet and Benny Goodman's bands. I have always carried two clarinets, keeping one as a back-up. They are very sensitive instruments. The reeds are easily damaged.

The biggest problems for wind instrumentalists, however, are not the instruments themselves but rather their teeth. In the old days, the loss of an instrumentalist's teeth could mean the end of his career. The best example of this was the great cornettist Bunk Johnson. When he had his front teeth extracted he had to give up playing. Years later, when some impresario wanted to recreate the jazz of New Orleans he found Bunk driving a lorry. He paid an orthodontist to build Bunk a set of false teeth and he managed to resurrect his career.

I encountered a big problem when my own teeth were extracted. Luckily Dr Al Vollmer, manager of the Harlem Blues and Jazz Band, a band I have played with for over a quarter of a century, is himself an orthodontist and he gave me some good advice.

I didn't realise at the time how lucky I was to meet Louis. The Musicians' Union was not that prepared to allow American bands to come over because they believed they were denying work to British bands. The union then compromised and allowed some of them to come over in exchange for bands like the Beatles being allowed to play across the Atlantic. That's how Duke Ellington appeared at Cardiff. Again I managed to make it backstage and spoke to the Duke. He explained in detail to me his philosophy regarding arranging chords.

Ellington's band was all black, as was Count Basie's band. Members of white and black bands were segregated socially, no drinking together, no eating together. Their relative musical styles were also completely different. Louis and Ellington, although their interpretations of jazz differed, drew from the same sources. The white bands drew their interpretations from totally different sources.

As in the case of Ellington, it was at Cardiff that I met Basie. He was with his guitarist, Freddie Green at the time. Unlike Ellington and Louis, Basie had nothing much to say. Not that he was unfriendly, he was just naturally reticent. He would much rather allow his fingers do the talking. Even so, I managed to chat with him and Green backstage.

I also met Basie in London. I was staying with a solicitor friend, Gilmour Evans, in the same hotel as Basie and his band. There is an old saying that suggests that solicitors can't play jazz. This was not true of Gilmour. He was a fine guitarist and banjo player. While we were in the reception area, Basie's bus drew up outside. The band members immediately rushed for the telephones to phone in their horseracing bets to the bookies. Basie had a large band so all the phones were immediately engaged. He had five saxophones, three trumpets, two trombones, piano, bass, drums and guitar. His music was based on the Kansas jazz tradition.

In the Maendy at Cardiff I managed to meet trombonist Jack Teagarden. Jack had played with Louis. He was the exception as he was white. When he formed his own band, he included black musicians. In fact it was my mentor Harry Parry that had first broken with convention by including black instrumentalists in his band. He smashed the taboo that insisted that bands should either consist of all white or all black musicians.

But to return to my teaching career. After a year in Loughborough, I was able to return to Pontyberem. This was convenient as it was close enough for me to travel from Mam's house daily. This was when I formed a jazz club in Llanelli. This was a landmark as it was not only the first jazz club in Llanelli, it was also the first jazz club in Wales.

Despite having spent time away from home I had managed to master both the clarinet and the piano and had started, with Mervyn, to learn the vibraphone. The vibraphone (or vibes) is a percussion instrument that sounds like a set of bells, similar to the xylophone only the hammers in this case are used to hit aluminium keys rather than wooden ones. It was popularised by artistes such as Milt Jackson, Lionel Hampton and Tubby Hayes.

The club started off in 1954 at the Half Way and then we moved to the Dock Hotel before moving on again to the Scouts' Hall. We

*Members of my first band in the Half Way in 1954: my brother Mervyn (piano),
me, Peter Lewis (drums), Graham Davies (trumpet) and Mel Guy (trombone)*

kept moving. There was the Cleveland, then the Melbourne, the
Mansel and then the Stepney. Wherever there was a good piano that
was in tune we would play there. There weren't all that many pianos
in Llanelli in those days that would qualify.

I now formed my first band, the Celtic Jazz Band, and I also
joined the Musicians' Union. Our line-up was based on the classic
New Orleans traditional jazz bands. Members of the first band were
Glan Clark on piano with Douglas Evans, a policeman, on bass,
Gareth Evans on guitar, my brother Mervyn on trombone, my old
pal Hamilton Davies on trumpet, Peter Lewis on drums and myself
on clarinet. We were soon given some good publicity. Ruth Parry
from HTV filmed us in a show at the Stepney and we also had a show
recorded at the Melbourne by Nuala Morgan, an Irish producer who
was married to rugby legend Cliff Morgan.

The Stepney was the ideal location. We played in the large
reception area in front of the huge dividing stairs. It grieves me to
know that the place has been demolished. It was once one of
Llanelli's most imposing buildings.

At the Stepney I also launched the jazz conventions that
preceded the various jazz festivals. My old mate from the Navy, Jim
Frost, brought his band from Southampton and friends from Brecon
brought their own band along. Friends from Swansea also brought

*The Celtic Jazz Band back in the 60s: Stafford Bowen (bass),
Brian Evans (piano), me, Peter Owen (trumpet),
Dave Cadwallader (drums) and Joe Pearce (trombone)*

their band. At the Ritz we organised dances with the profits going to
the Musicians' Union charging one and sixpence per head.

All three of us brothers were playing regularly by now. Mervyn
played both the piano and trombone in my band. Alwyn on the other
hand played solo, specialising in classical music on piano. He was the
most gifted amongst us. His son Alan now plays piano in my band.

Having established ourselves as a band we now concentrated on
developing our own style. And that style was swing. There was a
famous tune entitled 'It Don't Mean A Thing if it Ain't Got that
Swing'. Swing had been introduced to Britain during the 1940s by
Harry Parry. We began playing New Orleans style. And the band's
line-up was also based on New Orleans bands, but with clarinet
rather than sax, of course. This was the kind of jazz adopted by
British bands such as Ken Colyer, Terry Lightfoot and Acker Bilk.
This was the style we used when we made the semi-final of a radio
inter-counties talent show presented by Alun Williams on radio.
Among the tunes we played was 'Anchors Aweigh'. This was light
traditional jazz compared to Louis Armstrong's more classical style.
The band members at this time were Peter Owen (trumpet), Joe
Pearce (trombone), Brian Evans (piano), Dave Cadwallader
(drums), Doug Evans (bass) and myself on clarinet.

Turning to swing meant adopting a stronger rhythm section. Contemporary bands were getting rid of their string instruments and putting more emphasis on horns and other wind instruments. Once during his radio show Bing Crosby asked Louis Armstrong to explain swing. Louis replied, 'Ah! Swing! Well, we used to call it ragtime, then blues, then jazz. Now it's swing. Ha! Ha! White folks yo' all sho is in a mess!'

Of course, we would often be asked to play orthodox dance music such as waltzes, quicksteps and cha-cha-cha at various dances. This we would consider as a job of work when we would appear as the Wyn Lodwick Orchestra. This was bread and butter work. Jazz, on the other hand, was much more than a mere job of work. It was a pleasure.

Whichever the style, the response was always great with the venues always packed. Before we started playing live, the only jazz events of note were record clubs where aficionados gathered to listen to jazz records. Now for the first time we provided live jazz. We would perform at the jazz club and at dances throughout west Wales.

The Celtic Jazz Band in the Drill Hall, Llanelli, in April 1963.
Brian Evans (piano), Doug Evans (bass), me, Mario Lupi (drums),
Peter Owen (trumpet), Mervyn Lodwick (trombone) and Gareth Evans (guitar)

*The band in Pontarddulais in the company of politician Dennis Healy,
a great jazz fan, and his brother Peter*

Locally we would be asked to play at the Mayor's Ball, schools'
reunion dances, the Police Ball and similar events. Further afield we
would appear regularly at venues like the Victoria Hall at Lampeter
and at the Ivy Bush at Carmarthen.

Hospital dances were very popular back then and we played
regularly when they were held at Swansea, Treforest and
Carmarthen. On such occasions we would dress formally in suits,
white shirts and dickie bows. But we were ready to play anywhere on
any occasion from grand formal balls to Young Farmers' Club dances
in village halls.

Some venues gained bad reputations as roughhouses but we
never once had occasion to complain or fear. Indeed, jazz events
were all friendly, if perhaps high-spirited. Maybe jazz audiences were
more discerning. I don't know. Some so-called respectable people
thought jazz to be unseemly and uncivilised. Later, the same
accusations were levelled at rock and roll. To some it seemed to be
alien music. And of course it was thought of as black man's music.
Uncivilised, indeed!

When Mervyn taught at Coleshill School he felt rather
uncomfortable when appearing in public playing jazz. The

headmaster, Glanville Williams, was a deacon and Mervyn wasn't overly keen in drawing attention to the fact that he played in a jazz band. Therefore, when he performed he tended to skulk on stage as close to the wings as possible close to the curtains.

And rock, of course, suffered the same discrimination. There were widespread protests when the film 'Rock Around the Clock' appeared in Britain at the end of the Fifties. My quarrel with rock and roll is that in our case it killed our jazz club. One night in the Melbourne we were asked to make way to give a local band, the Corncrackers, the opportunity to play. They were the forerunners of the rock group Man. Following that show all the young people turned to rock.

We persevered, however, and often the unexpected happened. One night we were appearing in Laugharne while on the same night Dylan Thomas' Under Milk Wood was being performed by a company produced by Gwynne D Evans. Suddenly we were joined on stage by Drs Terry James and Wyn Morris. Terry was by then a well-known conductor while Wyn, who was one of my old school friends was an expert on Mahler. They had come to Laugharne to see the play but finished off jamming with us on stage.

One Christmas we were booked to play a gig at Brechfa. The weather, however, had turned bad with heavy snowstorms. Still, we decided to travel and the various band members were picked up, including bass player Hubert Hughes. His upright bass was always carried in a small trailer. We made it to Brechfa but the hall was in darkness. No-one expected us to turn up. Unknown to us, the place had been cut off for days.

I decided to call in the rectory to see the local vicar, the Rev Eric Gray. He immediately ran around the village informing everyone that the band had turned up. The hall was so cold that we had to place a small electric heater inside the piano to warm it. Despite everything, the dance went very well. At the end I offered the vicar a drink, thinking he'd ask for tea or coffee. Instead he asked for a whisky, a large one. He deserved it.

On another occasion we were due to play at the Victoria Hall at Lampeter. Again there had been a heavy snowfall. Our drummer, Dave Cadwallader, had travelled ahead earlier. We set off after him but by the time we reached Carmarthen the snow had even covered

Wyn Lodwick and his Quartet back in the early 60s: Brian Evans (piano), Hubert Hughes (bass), me, and Alwyn Davies (guitar). The drummer is Roger Brain, a former student of mine.

the engine. We had to abandon the car in Carmarthen and travel back to Llanelli by train leaving Dave on his own in Lampeter.

The band was fortunate in its characters. There was Elwyn Davies from Loughor, who played tenor sax occasionally. His brother Bill played bass. Elwyn was blind, and one day I called at his home to inform him of a gig. His wife answered the door and told me that Elwyn was round the back. I could hear the sound of an electric saw, and when I went round the back, there was Elwyn casually sawing logs with a circular saw.

The band members were ordinary chaps. But sometimes we would be joined on stage by other jazz players. One famous instrumentalist who joined us was the trombonist George Chisholm. George was a Glaswegian who was a clown as well as a serious instrumentalist. He had a very funny face and was a natural comic. He joined us on stage when we performed at the Orangery at Margam. George kicked off his career with the Royal Air Force Dance Band before he went on to form the Squadronaires, a band that became very famous after the war. He went on to record with giants like Fats Waller and Benny Carter. He was also a permanent member of the popular television series The Black and White Minstrel Show.

I should also mention jazz singer George Melly, who settled on the banks of the Wye. He often joined us on stage flamboyantly dressed in Twenties and Thirties American gangster style. He was a very colourful character who joined the Navy because he believed it boasted the smartest uniform of all the armed forces. He started off singing in Vaudeville style with Mick Mulligan and his Magnolia Jazz Band. He also worked with Wally Fawkes, another famous jazzman who was also responsible for the Flook cartoons in the Daily Mail. After a break from the stage for a number of years he returned in the 1970s with John Chilton's Feetwarmers and with the Digby Fairweather Band. Even though he was openly gay, George married twice.

We were privileged to appear with many famous bands of the time. Among them were Johnny Dankworth, Ken Colyer, Acker Bilk, Chris Barber and Alex Welsh, as well as blues pianist Champion Jack Dupree. This was when traditional jazz broke into the pop charts and

With my present band – Jeff Salter (tenor sax), Arthur Perry (drums), my nephew Alan Lodwick (piano) and Ron Davies (bass)

many of them appeared at Llanelli's Market Hall. However, this upsurge in the popularity of trad became a double-edged sword. Kenny Ball's 'Midnight in Moscow' and Acker Bilk's 'Stranger on the Shore' were not in fact jazz tunes but rather commercial hits. Bilk's band was far too good for this commercialisation. Yet I can see why he and others turned to commercial music. They had to make a living; unfortunately, though, they are now remembered for these hits rather than for their classical traditional tunes. 'Petite Fleur' by the Chris Barber Band with Monty Sunshine on clarinet was an exception. That tune, composed by Sidney Bechet, is itself a classic and deserved all the success it enjoyed.

The move from traditional to pop jazz was, therefore both a blessing and a curse. The blessing was the way that popular songs played in trad style found new jazz converts. The curse was that trad jazz became diluted and became pop music. This, in turn, was a turn-off for many true jazz aficionados.

Louis Armstrong and other giants were not immune to this trend. Ask anyone to name one of Louis' hits and you will be sure to hear either 'Hello Dolly' or 'What a Wonderful World' mentioned. In fact these are among his worst tunes. But they became popular among people generally. I'm sure that Louis performed and recorded such tunes against his better judgement.

Harry Parry, however, was still my mentor. And I feel rather ashamed for the way he has been neglected here in Wales. I learned a lot about him from his mother, Jane. He was born the eldest of five children in 1912 and was named Owen Henry. His father, who was a railway worker, was also named Henry. Harry attended Glanadda Primary School and then the local Central School. There, his headmaster prophesised in an end of term report that young Parry would become a great musician. He left school to work in the Physics Department at Bangor University. He had already joined a brass band when he was twelve and he was a member of St Mary's Church Choir. He quickly mastered the tenor horn, the flagella horn, the cornet, the violin and the drums, but concentrated mainly on the saxophone.

The drums, however, proved to be a problem. According to his mother, he played so loudly that they had to move house. So as not to disturb his new neighbours he would practise on the mountain side near St Mary's College. He found a tutor in Francis Jones of Port Dinorwic. He began performing publicly at the Powys Hall, Bangor and at Payne's Café in Llandudno as a member of Eddie Shaw's band. He was discovered by Percival Mackey and was invited to play at the Potomac Club in London where Mackey had his own quintet that included the blind pianist George Shearing among them.

It was on one of Harry's radio programmes that I was first introduced to Scott Joplin's music. The general public did not know of Joplin until 1973 when 'The Entertainer' became popular as the theme tune of the popular film *The Sting*. Incidentally, I have recorded the opening notes of 'The Entertainer' as the ring tones on my mobile phone.

Someone who had influence in the BBC heard Harry play and he was asked by Charles Chilton to form his own band. He also suggested that Harry should play the vibes. He first appeared on *Radio Rhythm Club* with his sextet on 28 September 1940. He also appeared regularly on *Anything Goes*.

I was thrilled to hear that Harry and his band were to appear at the Empire in Swansea. Alwyn drove me down there. I was only fifteen then. I managed to obtain the autographs of Harry and all the band members – Sam Molyneaux on bass, Dave Wilkins on trumpet, Ken Oldham on tenor sax, Joe Deniz on guitar, Sid Raymond on drums and Yorke de Souza on piano. When I approached Harry at the stage door he asked me where I came from. I told him I was from Llanelli and sang 'Sosban Fach' with him. He was delighted.

Dave Wilkins and Yorke de Souza were former members of Ken 'Snake-hips' Johnson's band, all of them Caribbean. The band was playing at the Café de Paris in London in September 1941 when a German bomb crashed through the cinema above, killing Johnson and other members as well as a number of the audience. Wilkins and de Souza survived and Harry invited them to join his band. This was one of the first instances of a white band including black musicians. Fifty years later I met de Souza at a gig in London. No-one but myself had turned up to listen to him. He was unknown. I spent the whole evening in his company.

Harry developed a style based on Artie Shaw and Benny Goodman. It was great to hear fresh music like his with tunes like 'Rock it Out' and 'Potomac Jump'. Those two tunes were on the very first Harry Parry record I ever bought. His music was unlike the music played by the dance bands of the time. He opened doors for me by introducing on his radio programmes music by giants such as Louis Armstrong, Bix Beiderbeck and James B Johnston. He was ranked, together with Frankie Weir and Carl Barriteau, as the greatest clarinettist in the world. Indeed, this was written in his obituary in the *Evening Standard* after he died.

During the war he travelled widely, entertaining the troops in the Middle East, including Egypt. His brother Tommy was killed at Monte Casino. He then formed his own permanent orchestra at the Potomac Club in London. His compositions 'Parry Opus', 'Thrust and Parry', 'Potomac Jump', 'Blues for Eight' and 'Says You' became very popular. The most popular of all was 'Champagne'. He adopted it as his signature tune. Harry appeared in five films and he was known as the British King of Jazz. He performed in venues all over the United Kingdom such as the Hippodrome in Birmingham, the Empire in Woolwich, and the Empire in Glasgow.

One of Harry's greatest fans was Spike Milligan. Spike himself had played jazz on trumpet until he encountered problems with his lips. He then turned to guitar and played with the Bill Hall Trio. Spike hated modern jazz and once said during an interview in Australia in 1970 how he was disillusioned with the progressive jazz played at the Number One Rhythm Club. 'Harry Parry, the clarinettist, came down one week,' he said, 'and that was like a visit by one of the gods.'

Harry continued performing at the Potomac throughout the bombing. But when the St Regis Hotel, where he also appeared regularly, was bombed he was forced for a while to work in a factory before he resurrected his sextet when the war was over.

I should also refer to an event held at the Stoll Theatre in 1941 when what was billed as The First English Public Jam Session was held. The session was recorded and I still have my copy of that record. On it Harry and his sextet play 'Honeysuckle Rose' backed with 'I Found a New Baby'. These songs are among the classics of jazz.

Harry unfortunately suffered badly with asthma and that's why he moved to India to a more suitable environment for a while. And jazz changed at an inappropriate time for him. By the end of the

1940s, Minton's in New York had become the heart of jazz. From there a more modern wave, known primarily as bebop, reached the shores of Europe, and Britain in particular. Be-bop had a higher tempo with the emphasis on the impromptu and based on a harmonic structure rather than melody. The bands were based on one or two saxophones, trumpet, bass, drums and piano with a guitar or strings sometimes added for good measure.

This kind of music, begun at Minton's, greatly influenced many of the hitherto traditional bands. It was at Minton's that Charlie Parker and Thelonious Monk became famous. The change reached the BBC's Jazz Club. The programme now included a half hour of traditional jazz and a quarter hour of modern jazz.

Towards the end of Harry's life, traditional jazz moved into pop. He died before he could reap the benefits. After he died I visited Caellepa to speak to his mother and sister. I also visited another of his sisters, Eunice, who lived in Essex. She had named her house 'Sŵn y Gwynt' ('The Sound of the Wind').

The titles to some of Harry's tunes were in Welsh or partly Welsh. Among them was 'Dim Blues' (no blues). And Dill Jones appeared with him. Harry's name was famous throughout the United Kingdom. He played regularly at locations such as the Locarno, the St Regis Hotel and at Jigs Club in London where he performed with such stars as Michael Flome, Louis Levy, Percival Mackey and Charles Shadwell. He, together with George Shearing and drummer Ben Edwards formed a very successful trio. But it was his sextet that really made him, with Joe Temperley on sax and musicians such as Tommy Pollard on vibes and piano, Lauderic Caton on guitar and Dave Wilkins on trumpet appearing with them. They recorded a disc on the Super Rhythm Parlophone label. He continued recording on that label for ten years resulting in classics such as 'I've Got You Under My Skin' with his octet and 'Mood Indigo' and 'Night and Day', with Dorothy Baronne as vocalist.

By the end of his career Harry had turned to the big band sound like Glenn Miller's, and appeared regularly on television with stars such as Eamonn Andrews, who presented the children's series *Crackerjack*, and on radio *Housewives Choice*. Harry's various foreign visits and his time in India especially took their toll and he was largely forgotten by the media. Yet, when he died in 1956 he was on the verge of a comeback. He was twice married, to Gwen Davies, and to Jessie Bradbury, who was a singer. But both marriages failed. He died, childless, at Adam's Row in London and his ashes were interred at Golders Green Crematorium. He and Sir Hugh Wheldon are regarded as the two most notable personalities to come out of Bangor during their time. There is a Harry Parry Archive at the University Library at Bangor. And at last there is a plaque on Harry's old home at Caellepa.

Harry was the greatest influence on our band in Llanelli. We were only a part of a much larger scene, of course. Llanelli catered for all kinds of music. I well remember Sir Adrian Boult performing at the Market Hall, or the Butter Market, as it was called. Butter was sold there during the day, then the place would be cleared for various performances. There was no permanent stage there, but a temporary stage would be installed when needed. It was there that the great singing festivals held by the various religious denominations were held. The material for the stage was usually lent by a local builder. After Sir Adrian Boult had performed with the London Symphony Orchestra a local Councillor stood up to propose a vote of thanks. He stood there proudly and said: 'Well, ladies and gentlemen, it gives me great pleasure to thank, first of all, Mr Boult. Thank you very much, Mr Boult, for bringing your band along. And thank you all in the audience for coming here tonight to this lovely concert. And before I finish I would like to thank Isaac Jones for the loan of the planks.'

The jazz club was not the only club I formed at Llanelli. I also formed the Llanelli Hockey Club. We would travel far and wide to play – up to Aberystwyth where we would be hammered by the University team. The same thing would happen in Cardiff. Then we would perhaps go to Haverfordwest, where we would occasionally win.

Following the year I spent in Loughborough I began working at the Education Centre at Pontyberem. Neil was now being looked after by Mam so I was able to live at home as well, travelling daily. And I stayed at Pontyberem until 1957. I was replaced at Trelech, coincidentally, by my brother Mervyn.

During my time there I was able to witness first-hand how the

Germans were coping after the war. I went out there with a party of musicians, among them Archie Clarke, a pianist who also played organ and accordion. It was an exchange visit. A party of German children had visited Pontyberem and now it was the turn of Pontyberem children to visit Germany. We accompanied them. We stayed with the local people and I was billeted with a former U-Boat Commander. He was a very influential man. His submarine had been captured during the war and he had spent time as a prisoner of war. Despite past hostilities he presented me with a clock as I left. With the clock he handed me a personal note to give to the customs officers authorising me to be allowed to keep the gift. This again proved to me that former adversaries could become friends.

Not everyone showed so much compassion. Our group had organised a concert over there but no-one turned up. To them we were still the enemy. Yet I couldn't complain. Driving through the outskirts of Hamburg we witnessed the after-effects of the blanket bombing the allies had carried out. One side of the city was flattened following air attacks and the Russian advance.

From 1957 to 1966 I taught at Gorseinon Further Education College. I was now a lecturer in engineering. There I found the curriculum was based more on the needs of industry. I would take mining trainees to art exhibitions and organise exhibitions at the college as well. Meanwhile, the band still performed.

Then, I was given the opportunity of combining education and jazz. I was appointed by Carmarthen Education Authority as Warden of the Community Education Centre at Pwll. The place was ideal. It had a hall with its own stage and the first thing I did was to add to the facilities to make it possible to organise concerts there. The Celtic Jazz Band was still performing and we took advantage of this perfect facility.

At the same time I organised craft courses at Ferryside and I added jazz officially to the curriculum. I then organised weekend courses leading to a concert at the end of the course. At Pwll I formed a ticket plan that allowed aficionados to enjoy cheese and wine with their music. To all intents and purposes this was the Llanelli Jazz Club newly born.

It was an additional bonus to me to be able to persuade Dill Jones and Clyde Bernhardt, who had been the trombonist with the Jelly

Roll Morton band from the 1920s, to perform there. Yes, jazz and education were now as one.

Chapter 4

If Harry Parry was my hero and mentor, my best friend in the world of jazz – both professionally and socially – was Dill Jones. Our paths had crossed in 1945, though neither of us realised it at the time. When I was sent to Skegness after I joined up, in May 1944, Dill called there – he had also joined the Navy – on his way to Ceylon, or Sri Lanka as it is known today. But years would pass by before we were to actually meet. Eleven years, as a matter of fact.

Before recalling our times together and our close friendship, I should write something of his background. He was born at Newcastle Emlyn on 19 August 1923 and named Dillwyn Owen Paton Jones, a grand-sounding name for such a modest fellow. As his father Islwyn was a bank manager with Barclays, the family moved around more often than most families. Dill was raised at Talgarth and then at Llandovery. Islwyn was from New Quay, where his father, D. O. Jones, was a minister. He was also a proficient photographer and some of the photographs he took are still to be found.

It would be true to say that New Quay was Dill's spiritual home throughout his life. His parents would take him and his sister Barbara there on holiday regularly. And towards the end of his life, it was to New Quay that he fled when the 'hiraeth' would descend on him in America. The English word 'longing' doesn't begin to describe the depth of feeling conveyed by the Welsh word 'hiraeth'. Dill believed that 'hiraeth' was akin to the black people's blues. His mother, Lavinia was a skilled pianist and she, together with Emlyn Evans, a teacher from Llandeilo, were his early tutors. He was a quick learner, and at only seven years of age he was playing Rubenstein.

At Llandovery, Bank House, where the Jones family lived, stood between two chapels. And I am convinced that the hymns he would regularly hear influenced him and his music, pointing him towards jazz. I have always maintained that a hymn tune such as 'Cwm Rhondda' holds the same depth of feeling as the blues. Dill would often compare Welsh 'hwyl' to black soul. And he freely admitted that hymn tunes heard as a child did, as we all suspected, play an important part in his musical development. He had also been impressed by the Gymanfa Ganu, a religious singing festival. He would probably have attended such musical events at New Quay where his aunt, Isawel Jones, was accompanist at Tabernacle Chapel. She would coach Dill musically at her home in Park Street. Isawel was his favourite aunt. She would ensure that he attended chapel on Sundays. But Dill, more than once, confessed that religious services always made him feel sad.

Back in the 1920s and 30s, New Quay was the favourite holiday destination for the Gwendraeth valley miners and their families. Often on warm summer evenings they would congregate on the quay to sing hymns. And no doubt, Dill would have witnessed such evenings. And the sea, of course. It was a big influence on his character and his music, and the rhythms and sounds of the sea are in his work. When he was called up to serve in the armed forces in 1942, it would have been natural for him to join the Navy. Later, of course, he performed as a musician on ocean liners. The sea was in his blood. He was descended from a host of sailors and sea captains. And the sounds and rhythms of the sea are reflected in his music. And it was either in the sea or on it that he spent his summer holidays, swimming and boating. Later, he performed on a ship crossing the Atlantic Ocean.

Dill was non-political party-wise. He has been described as a socialist who was also a Welsh nationalist. I would rather say that he was a Welsh nationalist who was also a socialist. Whenever he felt that Wales was being given a raw deal in any way, he would rage. And when he was sent as a day pupil to Llandovery College, I have a feeling that it was against his better nature. He must have felt, as a pupil in a public school, like a fish out of water.

Despite this, he managed to achieve what his parents expected of him. At Llandovery College he gained his certificate as well as achieving success in Latin and in Military Officers' Training. But far more important was the fact that it was at Llandovery, according to his sister Barbara, that he discovered jazz. I must have spent many hours discussing Dill with her at her home at New Quay. Barbara married the distinguished concert pianist Leonard Cassini, who considerably influenced Dill.

According to Barbara, as soon as her brother had managed to gain the minimum passes he needed, jazz took over his life. Not just any old jazz but jazz of a very high standard. He became the centre of attention, with other students crowding around the piano when he played in the common room. Apparently, he was so much at home playing jazz that he might well have been playing in his crib. From the very beginning, according to Barbara, his harmonising and his sense of rhythm were perfect, the result of constant practising.

Dill shared the opinion that the Welsh took to music naturally. He thought it was an integral part of our being. What the Welsh lacked, he thought, was a natural feeling for rhythm. Unlike black people, rhythm was not an innate gift to the Welsh. During those early years I believe that Dill felt lonely and frustrated. Yes, he had a ready audience, but he had no-one that could really share his new-found love. The college staff, in particular, had little enthusiasm in sharing his interest. Indeed, the college did not even include a music department. It is reported that the Principal, discovering Dill playing jazz on the piano, sadly shook his head and commented, 'No good will come of this boy.'

On Wednesday afternoons, the traditional games period, other boys would be out playing rugby leaving Dill alone playing the piano. His only sporting interest was boxing. And he was a skilled boxer, although his typical pugilistic nose suggested otherwise. Even during his latter years he would still instinctively raise his left hand to his nose in a defensive stance.

By his mid teens, Dill was totally infatuated with jazz. He had discovered Thomas 'Fats' Waller, having heard him on the few jazz programmes broadcast over the radio. Fats toured Britain in 1938, spending a whole week appearing at the Swansea Empire. Dill, being only fifteen years old at the time, did not see him, but Fats, undoubtedly was the most influential musician in his life during his early years.

Fats was a great exponent of stride playing, and composed classics such as 'Honeysuckle Rose' and 'Aint Misbehavin''. He is still regarded as a legendary jazz giant. His life was as flamboyant as his playing. He was a ladies' man, and in 1926 he was kidnapped by two of Al Capone's henchmen. However, it was a friendly kidnap. He was taken to one of Capone's famous parties, and there he played for the mobster and his friends for three days and three nights. He died when he was only twenty-nine years old. But boy, did he live!

Dill left Llandovery College at fourteen and found a job as a bank clerk. He quickly realised that working in a bank and jazz were hardly compatible. 'There is no purpose,' he said, 'in trying to balance the books when Bud Freeman's chorus from 'The Eel' keeps running through your head.' He left and joined the Navy in 1942 and set sail for the Indian sub-continent in 1945.

Like me, he spent time in Portsmouth, and there he was taught by the blind pianist Bill Cole. And again like me, life in the Navy broadened his experiences, both generally and in his musical education. Out in Sri Lanka he met Lennie Felix, and they played together on the British Armed Forces' radio network. Felix went on to form a trio with Lennie Bush on bass and Lennie Hastings on drums.

When Dill returned to Chatham in early 1946 he started appearing at the Red Barn at Barnehurst and in various clubs and pubs. He sometimes appeared in a duet with Cyrill Ellis on trumpet. They were known as Dai and Cy. He then joined The Melody Mariners, based at Peterborough. He met many up and coming jazzmen including Tommy Whittle, Alan McDonald, Arthur Greenslade and Ronnie Verrell.

At the end of his national service period he returned to work as a bank clerk at Westminster in London. As well as appearing in various London clubs he began contributing to the BBCs *Rhythm Club*. He then successfully applied for a grant to study at Trinity College, London, concentrating on the piano and the organ. But history repeated itself. As he had done at Llandovery College, he demanded that jazz came before all else. And once again, his obsession did not please his tutors. One afternoon as he played 'St Louis Blues' to a crowd of appreciative fellow students, one of his female tutors burst in and demanded to know what Dill was playing. He answered quite civilly, 'It's a piece by W. C. Handy.' She replied, 'We can't have music of that sort in a place like this.' Dill replied, 'Well, if that is the case, you won't have me here either.' He stood up and walked out, never to return.

His time at college was not wholly wasted, however. In London around this time he discovered the music of Louis Armstrong and Earl Hines, Lester Young and Jess Stacey. But he also acknowledged the genius of classical composers such as Ravel, Debussy, Beethoven,

Mozart and Poulenc. But as he grew older and matured, he increasingly turned to the pianist Bix Beiderbecke from Davenport, Iowa. Dill recorded a tribute record to Bix named 'Davenport Blues'.

Bix led a tragic life. He was a promising college academic when he decided to give it all up to play the piano and the cornet. His father was livid, but could not make his son change his mind. Bix turned increasingly to drink and when he returned home to recuperate, he was heartbroken to find that all copies of his recordings made over the years and sent by mail to his parents remained unopened. He died from the effects of alcoholism aged thirty-one.

It is probably true to say that Dill's musical career actually kicked off in May 1947 when he joined trumpeter and then clarinettist Humphrey Lyttelton, and drummer Carlo Krahmer, who went on to launch the Esquire label. Dill performed at the Nice Jazz Festival in 1948. There he saw Louis Armstrong in concert, a performance so beautiful that it made him cry. Dill was always emotional. At the festival he was invited to play with trombonist Jack Teagarden. Together they performed a tribute to Earl Hines, 'Caution Blues'. Hines had been a member of Louis Armstrong's band and was to rejoin him the following year as a member of Louis' All Stars.

That year, 1949, Dill performed at the Paris Jazz Festival with Vic Lewis' Orchestra, where he was bowled over by a performance by Charlie Parker. During his post-college period he also joined Harry Parry on tour through Holland and the Middle East. Harry's band, featuring Dill recorded 'I've Got You Under My Skin' and 'Blue Acara' in October 1949.

This was a formative year for Dill. He joined the BBCs Jazz Club and presented the programme on radio and on television throughout the Fifties. He was then invited, together with other musicians such as Ronnie Scott to perform in a quartet on the Queen Mary as it sailed between Southampton and New York. Crossing the Atlantic meant a five-day voyage. The pay was negligible but food and accommodation was gratis. What more did he need?

The bonus was that he could, on every voyage, spend two days ashore in New York while the liner was at anchor off 52nd Street. In the Big Apple he would visit the various jazz clubs, especially Eddie Condon's club, where he would often be invited to perform. He could now mix with pianists that had only been names in the past and enjoy their live performances. For the first time he could appreciate live performances by Coleman Hawkins: he was the first ever to utilise the tenor sax in jazz. Dill jumped at the opportunity of lessons by Lennie Tristano, a Chicago pianist famous for his avant garde style, a pioneer in the cool jazz style, be-bop and post-bop and a constant thorn in the side of the purists.

When Islwyn Jones retired from banking in 1955 and moved with his wife Lavinia to New Quay, this rekindled Dill's desire to visit as often as he could. In London, he moved to a flat in Westbourne Terrace near Paddington Station so that he could catch the train to Wales on a whim. And this he did regularly.

Sharing the flat with Dill was Tony Kinsey, drummer and composer, who went on to form the Johnny Dankworth Sextet. Dill joined Kinsey's group and also went back to playing classical music. His ambition was to raise jazz, as well as those who played it, to concert level. He saw jazz as a social art as well as being a musical art. Jazz, he believed, was the only true form of international folk music.

In 1953 he recorded his first solo album. He went on to record with Tony Kinsey and Tommy Whittle, and when Whittle left his quintet in 1955 Dill formed his own trio and signed a recording contract with Columbia and Polygon. Dill's trio and George Melly's band were the only British bands to appear at the Beaulieu Jazz Festival in 1956. At the Royal Festival Hall, at a concert in aid of the Hungarian people following the Soviet invasion, he played on the same stage as Louis Armstrong. He spent three days rehearsing with the great man. Dill and Louis performed Bernstein's arrangement of 'St Louis Blues', as well as performing a number of religious tunes and songs connected with Louis.

This was the time when Dill and I played together for the first time. It happened at the New Quay Yacht Club Ball held at Llanybydder in 1956, and little did I imagine at the time how significant that meeting would prove to be.

Although this was the first time for us to perform together, I had met him nine years previously when he appeared with the Harry Parry Sextet. Then, on the day of the Yacht Club Ball I called at Dill's parents' home, Illrousse, at New Quay for a chat. We discussed in particular Harry Parry's music and then jazz in general. This was when our friendship really began. Dill had agreed to play at

Llanybydder as a guest. I hired a grand piano from Swansea for £27.

Significant as that night was to prove, something else sticks in my mind to this day – the overpowering stench of Jeyes Fluid in the gents' toilet. Indeed, every time I think of Llanybydder, I still smell Jeyes Fluid. The smell of chop suey and chow mein is there now! The old Victory Hall has become a Chinese restaurant.

Dill's modesty was amazing. Straight from appearing at the Beaulieu Jazz Festival he had agreed to play with me at Llanybydder. It was his great modesty that endeared him so much with everyone he met. He loved people, and people loved him.

To me, one of his greatest attributes was his ability to cross borders. He would cross jazz boundaries with ease, jumping from classical to traditional and back again whenever the mood took him. He ceaselessly crossed geographical borders between London, America and Wales. And he also crossed that monstrous boundary that separated white from black with the same ease. In addition he was good company and a great talker on any subject under the sun. He would talk happily with anyone.

He was, if anything, too generous, too prepared to put his hand in his pocket when he thought someone was in need. Too ready to give free tuition to a would-be instrumentalist. His presence in a band would always raise the standard and the spirit of his fellow players. He was the inspiration to all around him.

Meanwhile, Dill's career flourished. He was on a roll. He was voted best pianist of the year by the influential weekly music newspaper *Melody Maker* four times in succession. He was described as 'an eclectic pianist', one that had succeeded in fusing two genres of jazz, the traditional and the mainstream while including modern idioms. This was at a time when jazz was being split by bigoted, stubborn so-called pundits.

Dill formed a new band, the Dill Jones All Stars, as well as the Dill Jones Orchestra and the Dill Jones Dixieland All Stars. The All Stars caused a stir when Dill and his fellow members, Vick Ash on clarinet and Keith Christie on trombone, played traditional jazz at the Flamingo Club. Many saw this as a retrograde step. Dill couldn't care less. He detested being categorised.

Despite being active as a live performer, he was experiencing a hiatus as far as recordings were concerned. But he did record an album that is a rarity today, called Jones the Jazz. Then he took to a new and unexpected hobby, gliding. Flying was something he loved.

The dearth of black musicians in British bands grieved him. British bands seemed to want to draw closer to the Europeans, while black bands adhered to soul and gospel. Dill had, by this time, encountered some of the black giants of jazz in New York, while in London he had met Louis. He had also met and recorded with Big Bill Broonzy and Joe Harriot, who promoted black music, as well as white bands like Chris Barber, who opened the door to black traditional music, attracting stars like Sonny Terry and Brownie McGhee to London jazz and folk clubs.

He came to a critical decision. He decided to settle in America. To a man like Dill who loved Wales this must have been a difficult decision to make. He wanted to go to America, he said, to research into black soul, or black 'hwyl', as he called it. In addition he was suspicious of the rise of rock and roll in Britain, seeing it as a threat to jazz. He also saw America as a land of opportunity, as many others before him had visualised it. He left in May 1961 and settled in New York. He wrote to me regularly once a week. He never missed. This, to me, was his way of overcoming the deep 'hiraeth' that he felt.

On the positive side he was happy in his exploration of all kinds of ethnic music. He visited Harlem, New York's jazz cradle, where he was taught by Luckey Roberts, a pianist who, together with James P Johnson, specialised in the 'stride' piano style. Roberts composed tunes such as 'Junk Man Rag', 'Moonlight Cocktail', 'Pork and Beans' and 'Railroad Blues'. Roberts stated that Dill was the finest white pianist he had ever encountered. That was some tribute.

Luckey Roberts had developed his own personal stride style, based on Fats Waller's percussion-like use of his left hand. It was said that Roberts' left hand could cover fourteen piano keys. It was rumoured that his uncanny ability in covering so many keys was the result of surgery that entailed splitting the flesh between his fingers down through his knuckles so that he could achieve the maximum span. This, however, was a rumour spread by jealous detractors. His hands were naturally, if unusually, large.

When the first-ever Welsh Jazz Festival was held in Cardiff in 1978, Dill exhibited his ability as a stride pianist with his version of 'Shim-me-sha-Wabble'. Yet he still found it difficult to break into black bands. So he had to be content with playing with white musicians at Condons, among them the trombonist Jimmy McPartland, trumpeter Yank Lawson and trumpeter and band leader Max Kaminsky. McPartland had served with American soldiers in Pembrokeshire back in 1943 during the preparations for D-Day.

Then Dill fell on hard times. Work became scarce and he was reduced to selling records and entertaining customers at Macy's department store and giving piano lessons. At the store he and a harpist performed under the name 'The Dragon and the Harp'. He was staying at the Hotel Wales in the Upper East Side near Central Park on Madison Avenue. Then came a big break. He was invited to join the Gene Krupa Quartet. Krupa was a world-famous drummer, born in Chicago of Polish parents.

Dill decided to visit New Orleans, the spiritual home of black jazz. Ultimately, in 1967 he broke into the black scene when he was invited to perform at the Manassas jazz festivals playing with established musicians such as Bill Pemberton, Oliver Jackson, Budd Johnson and Clyde Bernhardt. He also appeared with Willie 'The Lion' Smith and was invited to be a member of the JPJ Quartet, replacing Earl Hines, with Johnson, Jackson and Pemberton. They became an established band, travelling and playing throughout

Dill Jones, the maestro, tickling the keys

America including an appearance at the 1971 Montreaux Festival. As well as performing, they organised jazz workshops attended by a total of 70,000 children from schools from all over America. His one disappointment was the lack of interest among record companies.

Dill left the JPJ Quartet in 1973 and for the next eleven years he mainly performed solo. He was coming over to Wales once a year and was insistent that I should go back with him. And early in 1973 I succumbed to his pleadings. I travelled alone, however, catching an Aer Lingus flight from Heathrow to Shannon and then to New York. At the airport I caught a bus and then a taxi to the Hotel Wales. Dill was out performing but behind the desk he had left his key and a message telling me he was appearing somewhere or other with the JPJ Quartet.

When I opened the door to his suite I was faced with a huge poster on the wall proclaiming, 'Croeso i Efrog Newydd, Wyn bach!' *(Welcome to New York, Wyn bach!).* And all round the bed he had arranged a display of records by every clarinettist I admired.

I soon learned that the old saying was true. Everything in America was bigger than anywhere else. One day the couple from next door invited me out for a day's fishing. I asked Dill whether I should, perhaps, take my coat with me. Little did I realise that we were to travel 129 miles to Montauk Point, the furthest piece of land on Long Island.

After one visit I travelled back with Dill. Before going to the airport I called with him at a studio called Warehouse D, where he recorded a Fats Waller tune, 'Up Jumped You With Love'. I remember walking with him along Oxford Street. On the pavement in front of us was an empty milk bottle. Dill made a big issue of this. It was dangerous, he said. Who could have been so foolish as to leave a bottle on the pavement? After pontificating for some time he picked up the bottle and placed it carefully on a doorstep, cursing whoever it was that had left it. Little things like that bugged him.

He moved from the Hotel Wales to a bed-sit in East Village on East 12 Street, a rough area of the city. Next door there was a bar run by a hard-headed lady known as Slugger Ann. Every window in every building was protected with iron bars and every door was fortified with double locks. Dill's apartment consisted of one room and a small bathroom. All he had in the flat was a table, two chairs, a bed, piano, filing cabinet, and recording and playing equipment. When I called he would give me his bed.

But the iron bars and double locks were not enough. One day we left the apartment together. When we returned someone had broken in and had stolen everything except for the larger items of furniture. Dill asked me to check the filing cabinet for the file labelled 'M'. I found it and opened it. Inside was $200. He had filed it under 'M' for Money! Dill's greatest loss was his precious collection of records. They were priceless, many of them personal and most of them irreplaceable.

On another occasion I was in the apartment on my own when I noticed smoke pouring out of a window in next door's apartment. I had no idea who lived there but I had heard the doorbell being rung regularly, day and night. I then realised that the smoke was coming from dry bushes below the window at the back of the building. I ran downstairs and out and rang next door's bell shouting loudly, 'Fire! Fire!' I then returned and looked out the window. And what a sight! Naked men and women were running to and fro carrying jugs full of water from the apartment and emptying them on the fire. What I didn't know was that the apartment was a brothel!

When Dill eventually left the apartment, it was taken up by Ram Ramirez, a remarkable Puerto Rican pianist who turned professional when he was only thirteen. He became a member of the Harlem Blues and Jazz Band and I played with him when we toured Belgium. The highlight of his career was composing 'Lover Man', a song that was recorded by Billie Holiday.

Occasionally I would join Dill on stage in New York. We played together at the David Copperfield at 1394 York Avenue on 35th and Lexington. We also played at the Van Dyck in Albany. There one night I saw Red Norvo performing there. I also saw Mildred Bailey singing there. A lady called Ardis Timmis would join us at the Van Dyck. Her husband was a close friend of President Gerald Ford. We once spent a few days at her home in East Greenbush out in the country.

It was there that I met two of Dill's friends called John and Pug Horton from Yorkshire. John was a doctor specialising in treating cancer. He played trombone in his own band, the Cellar Six. John would later play a leading part in Dill's fight against cancer. John and

I became good friends. I would visit him in Yorkshire and he would stay with me in Llanelli.

At New York, Dill would also appear regularly in The Windows on the World restaurant high up in the World Trade Centre on the North Tower, one of the twin towers destroyed on 11 September 2001 by terrorists. Dill took me there just before the Centre was opened in 1973. He took me up as far as the 34th floor of the North Tower. That was high enough for me. But the restaurant where Dill played with Jimmy Hamilton, who later played clarinet with Duke Ellington, was on the 107th floor. Ifor Rees from the BBC in Cardiff filmed Dill there as part of a Welsh-language documentary called 'Ar y Brig' *(on top)*. Neil and I once visited the restaurant when Dill was performing there. It was a strange experience looking down on the planes that flew past.

Towards the end of the Seventies, Dill and I were invited to perform on Cape Cod with the Harlem Blues and Jazz Band for the first time. The leader was Clyde Bernhardt. He was the trombonist and had played with King Oliver and Jelly Roll Morton. In fact, the band started life as Clyde Bernhardt and the Harlem Blues and Jazz Band. I became very friendly with Clyde and he stayed with me in

Jamming with members of the Harlem Blues and Jazz Band: George James (alto sax), Johnny Williams (bass) and Frank Williams (trumpet)

*Me with Candy Ross (trombone) and George Kelly (tenor sax)
from the Harlem Blues and Jazz Band*

Llanelli. The band was the brainchild of Al Vollmer, an orthodontist and a fanatical trad jazz historian, who lived in Larchmont near Westchester, north of New York.

Dill introduced me to the band. All the members were stars of the past, all of them black musicians apart from Dill and I. The only other white member to join the band was drummer Johnny Blowers. When I was asked to join as an honorary member I felt honoured. Dill was the exception as he was so much younger than the rest. He had only turned fifty-five when he joined. Max Lucas, on the other hand, who played tenor sax, played on with the band until he died at ninety-nine. Bill Dillard, who was King Oliver's ex-trumpeter, did not join until he was well in his eighties.

With the members being so old, there was inevitably much coming and going with constant changes in personnel. Every year when I joined them, there would be a missing face and a new face in his place. These musicians were incredibly experienced. Johnny Blowers had drummed for Tommy Dorsey and had backed Frank Sinatra for fifteen years, and had also backed Billie Holiday and Ella Fitzgerald. Pianist Sammy Benskin had also backed Ella Fitzgerald,

Billie Holiday and Sarah Vaughan. Vocalist Laurel Watson had fronted Duke Ellington's orchestra and recalled scandals involving her and Billie Holiday. Once they fought each other over a man. On another occasion during an argument, Billie attacked her with a broken bottle. I was honoured by accompanying Laurel on 'I'm Confessing', a number that was included on my CD *Fifty Years of Jazz*.

Another veteran was trumpeter Fred Smith, who had appeared with all the greats, from George Kelly to Aretha Franklin. Guitarist Al Casey had played with Fats Waller since 1935. Trombonist Candy Ross had backed Frank Sinatra, Sammy Davis Junior and Shirley Bassey. And Johnny Williams on bass had played and recorded with Louis Armstrong, as well as with all the other greats.

I would fly out to join the band at least once a year. And every time I did, I felt honoured. On my first visit we travelled from Larchmont up to Hopkinton, Massachusets. During the morning we appeared on television. On the night of our gig at the Sticky Wicket we had as vocalist Viola Wells, known as Miss Rhapsody. She specialised in swing and in blues singing. Members of the band on that occasion included George James, Johnny and Frank Williams,

Dill and me in the Stepney in Llanelli at the end of the 1970s

George James, drummer Tommy Benford and Dill on piano.

I shared a room with Johnny Williams, who became a close friend. That night before we slept, he played some of his records in the bedroom including one on which he sang 'Ole Rocking Chair' in Louis Armstrong's band. My brother Mervyn's daughter Catherine and her husband Emyr were living in Boston at the time and they both came over to see us playing.

Once in the Copley Plaza in Boston, Dill was appearing with the in-house pianist, Dave McKenna. Dave, like Dill, had been a member of Gene Krupa's band and had appeared with many of the top jazzmen. Dill was surprised to see the bartender coming over with a pint of beer for him. He looked over at the bar and there stood my cousin Terry James with actor Richard Harris. They were over in Boston with the cast of *Camelot,* which was playing in the city at the time.

The older he grew, the more of a Welshman Dill became. Being an exile in America made him more aware what he was missing back in Wales. He still went back to New Quay every year and I would travel with him and my band throughout Britain and Europe. He had always been unable to hide his accent. Not that he wanted to. And he would carry Welsh language books with him everywhere, reading them as an aid to polish his Welsh.

He had taken very much to Dylan Thomas' work. Both of them had strong connections with New Quay, of course. One of his favourite pieces was *Return Journey,* the author's autobiographical piece where Dylan the man returns to Swansea to try and find Dylan the child. He would ask me sometimes to read to him *A Visit to Grandpa's.* He felt that I possessed a Welsh accent that could do justice to the story. He admired Dylan not only as an author but also as a man who identified with the common people and despised the rich, especially when the author himself had been so poor.

I sometimes wonder whether the two ever met. He never mentioned it, so it seems unlikely. And that is strange because both of them were regulars at the Black Lion at New Quay where a great character, Jack Patrick, was the landlord.

Dill would often refer to his love for his Welsh inheritance, the landscape, the people, rugby and boxing, songs and pub life. And he was forever going on about improving his Welsh even though he was sharing his life between New York and London. He wasn't doing this for any sentiment or for his self-importance but because he loved the language and believed it to be a national treasure. He believed that a language that had survived for some fifteen centuries deserved to survive.

When we would meet in New York we would go to the bar of the Wales Hotel or some other bar where he enjoyed speaking very loudly in Welsh. He loved to see people turn to listen to two people conversing in a language that was totally strange to the rest. Nothing pleased him more that seeing someone come over to ask us what language we were speaking. This gave him the opportunity to talk of

Wales and things Welsh.

Once, when I arrived in New York he left me a message telling me that he was performing in a certain bar. I called a taxi and went there. He was there, engrossed in his performance during the 'happy hour'. He did not notice my arrival. Then, suddenly I heard the notes of the Welsh national anthem. He had spotted me and wanted to welcome me.

Like many performers he liked his drink. Usually he would drink a glass of beer with a Bourbon chaser. Then I began to notice that he ate very little. He did not appear as one who drank too much. Yet, after he died his doctor told me that Dill's kidneys were the size of cricket balls. He wasn't an alcoholic. I never saw him drunk. He drank to try and forget his loneliness. The only time that he was completely happy was when he was performing.

Towards the end of his life an element of 'hiraeth' entered his songs and tunes. It became evident in tunes such as 'Welsh Pearl', 'Blues Alone', 'New Quay News' and 'There Are No Flowers in Tiger Bay'. I remember him once appearing on Humphrey Lyttelton's programme being introduced as 'an English pianist'. He got annoyed and emphasised that he was not English, but Welsh. I was with him during a broadcast made from Albany when he explained that he was from Wales. He was most put out when the interviewer asked him, 'What sort of city is Wales?' It did not take Dill long to enlighten him.

In 1981 at a jazz conference in Australia, Dill realised for the first time that he had a serious problem with his throat. He had mentioned to me as I drove him to catch the train to the airport that he found swallowing difficult. The following year he returned to New Quay and visited his aunt Isawel. He was closer to her than he was to anyone else. Then we travelled to Llanrhystud where we recorded our album *Y Cyswllt Cymreig* (the Welsh connection), a collection of Welsh and black folk songs.

Dill then travelled to Berne where he was taken ill. But there he was told that there was nothing seriously wrong with his throat. Back in America he called on his old friend, Doctor John Horton, who diagnosed cancer. John rang me on Christmas Day 1982 enquiring whether I would be able arrange for Dill to be examined by a British doctor as it would cost him $144,000 to do so in America. I was with him when he flew home with the X-ray plates given to him in

America, and travelled on to New Quay. There we contacted an ear, nose and throat specialist, an old friend of ours, Doctor Gareth Williams at Glangwili Hospital, Carmarthen. Like us, Gareth was a sailing enthusiast. He soon realised that things were not good. He arranged for Dill to go to London for treatment that involved removing the voice box.

This was a terrible blow to Dill. He could still play the piano but his singing career was over. He loved to sing. He would sing anything from classics such as 'A Hundred Years From Today' to comic songs like 'I'm Henry the Eighth I Am, I Am'. Singing now was out of the question.

Following surgery, Dill stayed with Rosemary and myself at Pwll – I had re-married in 1976. He would spend his time playing the piano and gazing out over the Loughor estuary. Music and the sea, his two great loves. He visited New Quay for the last time, mainly to say goodbye to Isawel. Then he flew back to America. He moved out of his flat and stayed at the home of a girlfriend, Wendy Flannard, a widow, at Port Washington on Long Island. He began performing again for a while but he suffered a relapse and was taken to the Saint Vincent Hospital, where Dylan Thomas, one of his heroes, had died thirty years previously. Johnny Blowers visited him regularly.

In the depth of his illness I visited him for the last time in Port Washington. Another visitor was Dave McKenna. Dill was confined to his bed as Dave played some of the old tunes and reminisced. Dave himself died of cancer five years ago.

Dill's last letter to me was written in pencil in essay form, his writing still clear and firm. In it he asks me, 'a trusted friend', for advice. In it he reiterates his love for Wales and its people:

> Naturally, confusion has been a constant partner lately, but I've used up all the will and strength I have to fight back. Tell Jim and Ardis (Timmis) I long for the great times, the friendship, laughter and warmth we enjoyed together. I know the family and knowing them is one of my outstanding American experiences.
>
> I am often consumed by homesickness for Wales, and yet I know I could not turn back the pages of time. Wales is changing – everywhere! New generations (the law of life)

prevent the expatriate from realising the impossible dream. To return to the same people, atmosphere and "geography" even, is something unattainable. I am so fortunate to have so many friends in my dear Homeland.

I trust that I have made a reasonable success of my life (although not materialistically). And I don't think I made a wrong move in coming to the USA to improve my art. I never found security here and really I was never able to completely tear up my roots from Wales. Not even when I lived in London. This is a burden I have always had to bear. But look at all the friends I made and the experiences all over the world.

He went on to describe the sudden break-up of his health coming as a terrible shock:

Remember how full of energy I was? I don't think I was self-destructive and I was true to myself as much as I could be. I suspect that I am somewhat over-emotional and worrisome.

Even with my love for my native land, I am disturbed at times by the arrogance and snobbery some of the invaders have brought to it. I love the Wales and the Welsh of the Llanelli Cricket Club, the old Dolau and Black Lion of New Quay. The rough diamond quality of the valleys and the heartlifting wit and warmth of us all who sing the anthem with such amazing grace and power. The brave, compassionate quality of the Celt. The speed, grace and energy of the rugby football player and the blunt and rugged way of Colin Jones with Milton McCrory.

He then returned to his own career:

I have always hoped that I did something definite in advancing the interest in jazz culture in Wales as the music itself moved towards international recognition as a universal art form. Black culture I have always felt to have many parallels with that of Wales. I felt this very strongly when I first heard Paul Robeson.

He jotted down a few notes informing me that the sound of rain on the roof was a great comfort, an emotion he shared with W. C. Fields. And he referred to Dylan Thomas' *Visit to Grandpa's*, his favourite short story. In it, Grandpa has left home and is found on Carmarthen Bridge on his way to Llansteffan, where he wants to be buried. Dill noted that the last words of the story referred to Grandpa as 'a prophet who has no doubt'.

Dill died on 22 June 1984 in the Calvary Hospital in the Bronx. I was preparing for a television programme for HTV when I was told the news by the producer, Wyn Thomas. I found it very difficult to continue. But it was a live programme. There was no choice.

A memorial service was held at St Peter's Church on Lexington Avenue and 54th Street, and his ashes were scattered from the Verrazano Bridge, connecting Staten Island and Brooklyn. Later that year, at the Lampeter National Eisteddfod Dill was posthumously accepted as a member of the Gorsedd of Bards. He was honoured for the special musical aspect of his art as a musician who had succeeded in blending Welsh folk songs into his music.

Twenty years later a collection of thirty-one tunes on an album named *Davenport Blues – Dill Jones Plays Bix, Jones and a Few Others* was recorded. Without any doubt, Dill was the greatest jazz instrumentalist ever to be born in Wales.

Chapter 5

It is no surprise that I'm a Baptist. I have been on very friendly terms with water all my life. When I was a child I would often, apparently, open the tap in Mam-gu's greenhouse and splash water all over the place, mostly all over myself. But Mam-gu managed to put a stop to this. She tied a piece of wood to the tap and called it Bwm Bam. I was so frightened of the Bwm Bam that I never touched the tap again.

But it needed more than the Bwm Bam to keep me from seawater. I have constantly been either beside it, on it, or in it, all my life. When Mervyn and I were kids we would spend most of our playtime down the harbour. It was like a huge open play area for us, in those days long before Health and Safety regulations smothered fun like a wet blanket.

We would often go down with Uncle Ifor, and on the way we would call at Mr Rubenstein's jewellery shop in Station Road. Mr Rubenstein was a Jew who had a terrier called Rags. We would take Rags with us down to the harbour. There we would throw sticks and cans in the water and Rags would dive in like a seal and retrieve them. In the North Dock there was a swing bridge and there we would watch the small coasters sailing in and out, among them the *Afon Gwili* and the *Afon Lliedi*. In those days, little fishing boats would bob and weave their way in and out of the harbour surrounded by seagulls screeching like banshees. It is all so sadly quiet today.

Because Uncle Ifor was a Sanitary Officer he would board the boats and ships to check them in case they broke hygiene regulations. I would often take the opportunity of going with him. Not that Uncle Ifor was over-officious and wished to intrude: his main reason for boarding the various vessels was that he loved people and would chat till the cows came home.

Among the ships that fired the imagination was the *Polmanter*, a steamship that was, of course, coal-powered. I would always look forward to seeing it in the harbour. The biggest vessel I remember seeing there was the *Kajak*, that carried iron ore from Sweden to the local furnaces as well as pit props for the coalfields of the Gwendraeth Valley. It was so large that it took quite some skill to turn it within the harbour confines. She would leave with a cargo of coal and sheet steel. The sheet steel came from the local ironworks while the coal came from Pontyberem and Pont-henri along the railway line in trucks to the harbour.

One of my greatest adventures was the occasion when a dead whale was washed ashore at Second Slip, Pwll, the exact spot where Amelia Earhart had landed her sea-plane following her transatlantic flight in 1928. I was at the Regal cinema with Alwyn and our gang of friends when the rumour spread of a dead whale at Pwll. When the film was over, we all ran to the spot, a distance of around a mile and a half, where we saw the great leviathan dead on the beach. Some of the more adventurous boys attempted to extract one of the whale's teeth, but to no avail.

It is no wonder I am a sea-lover. Tad-cu was a seaman by nature, an occasional fisherman who would walk over eight miles to Cydweli to fish from a boat called the Paul. This was a German three-master that had been wrecked before the Great War off Cefn Sidan sands. It was salvaged and restored. The spot where it was discovered was near the Bertwn, where three rivers meet in an area called the Crow's Foot, because of the shape formed by the confluence of the three rivers.

Sometimes we would be allowed to go with Tad-cu and Mam-gu to Ferryside where we would be taken by boat across to Llansteffan. Occasionally this would be a part of our Sunday School trip. The trip itself would take us to Ferryside, and crossing the estuary to Llansteffan would be a bonus. The crossing itself would take around half an hour. There was room for around a dozen passengers. It was probably on this boat that I first went to sea.

I was also taken on the *Devonia*, a small paddle steamer that sailed out of Swansea. It left around six o'clock in the evening for the Scarweather lightship, a voyage of around two hours one way. We would travel to Swansea on one of the Bassett buses from Gorseinon. On one occasion Dad, Uncle Ifor, Alwyn and I were on the *Devonia* during a strong wind. It was so strong that the ship was unable to turn. In addition there was always a strong current in this channel between the Scarweather sand flats and Swansea. During the summer of 1819, a brig named the *George* sank there and eight crew members were drowned.

On the *Devonia* on that windy evening there were some frightened passengers. But Uncle Ifor had no worries. He was up on deck drinking red pop. At least, that is how he always described his tipple to me. I stood high in the middle of the top deck, the best place in a storm. It is always a great mistake to huddle down below in bad weather. On top and amidships is the place to be, where there is plenty of air.

Sometimes Mam-gu, when she saw from her window that there were white horses riding the waves, would try and persuade Uncle Ifor not to go. Mam-gu, naturally would be worried. But he wouldn't listen. Off he would go, and more often than not, he would take me and Mervyn with him.

Yes, the sea has always attracted and intrigued me from boyhood. I was raised on stories of Dad sailing out to war. Indeed, following the wounds he suffered at Ypres to both legs, leading to the amputation of one leg from below the thigh, his own father, Tad-cu Lodwick was allowed to sail out to see him at the war hospital. He was unconscious and no-one gave him much of a chance of surviving. As Tad-cu walked into the ward in his hobnailed boots, Dad recognised his step and woke up. And from that day he gradually recovered. I remember him repeating the words addressed to him by the surgeon who had operated on him: 'Lodwick, when they ask you who carried out this short-leg amputation, you tell them it was Major White of Dublin.' Obviously, he was pleased with his work.

I can also remember him telling me how he got around the censors when he wrote home. He would write in Welsh and in code. For instance, he would refer to 'braich mewn dagrau' (*arm in tears*) meaning, of course, that he was in Armentiers. Soldiers were forbidden to disclose their location.

When Mervyn and I were children, my parents could not afford to buy a boat. But Mervyn and I found a discarded old hulk rotting on the beach at Ferryside. It was obvious that no-one owned it. Mervyn and I therefore claimed it and we worked hard on making it seaworthy. And we succeeded. But after all the work we put in, even before we launched it, someone stole it. Still, we enjoyed the fun while it lasted.

Another trip we would enjoy was the short voyage from Tenby to Caldey Island and its monastery. It was just a hop, in fact. I continued the tradition after Neil was born. I remember taking him there when he was a boy. At the end of our visit the Abbot asked us whether we had any questions. Neil immediately asked him out of the blue whether the monks filled in the football pools coupons! An unexpected question, to say the least!

Then there was the *Lady Rowena*. This was a pleasure boat bought by a crew of local lads from Llanelli and anchored in the North Dock. They started organising shopping trips to Swansea and back on Saturdays. It would sail out past the Worm's Head and the Whitford lighthouse. (This, by the way was a metal structure, the only lighthouse of its kind in Europe.) Then she would sail on along the Gower coast and on to Swansea harbour where she would anchor while the passengers went shopping.

One Saturday, with Mam among the passengers, the ship started wallowing as it rounded the Worm's Head peninsula. The rumours that the ship was in danger of sinking reached Llanelli, and a crowd assembled at the North Dock, among them Tad-cu and Mam-gu. There were genuine concerns for the safety of the passengers and crew. Luckily, hours late, it made it home safely with no casualties. Today, incidentally, I can see the Worm's Head clearly from my lounge window, rising out of the sea like a primeval beast.

Later on, Mervyn bought his own boat, the *Marged*. This was a whaler-type boat, a 32-foot double-ender. It had a powerful diesel engine and was, therefore, a fast vessel. I helped him with the wood and metal work and with the painting. After restoring it, Mervyn decided to sell it. A crew of ten people became interested in buying it and Mervyn and I took them out on a trial run. Mervyn was crewing and I was up front.

We sailed out of Burry Port towards the Whitford lighthouse. With Mervyn steering, I happened to lift one of the forward hatches and realised that water was seeping in. How could I alert Mervyn without the prospective buyers realising there was something wrong? Once they realised she was shipping water, they would have little interest in buying it. So I addressed Mervyn nonchalantly, 'Mervyn, do you remember the *Lady Rowena*?' He immediately understood and told the potential buyers, 'Right, we'll turn back now.' It was touch and go, but we made it back to the harbour. We completely repaired it and successfully sold it.

The sea was as natural a part of everyday life to Mervyn and me, as natural as was the sky above us. In fact we regarded it as a neighbour, and a good neighbour at that. The sea was visible from Mam-gu's house. It was a natural feature, an integral part of the landscape. It also ran in my blood. That is why there was no question which arm of the Services I would join when I reached my eighteenth birthday (15 March 1945). I felt that the sea was somehow pure and cleansing. I also fancied the Navy uniform. It was so much more romantic than Army khaki or RAF light blue. It was therefore a natural step to take as I felt so comfortable at sea.

I had already been following a full-time six month radio course at Swansea's Radio Training College. At that time, of course, the Germans were regularly sinking British ships, and there was a dearth of officers. I therefore felt that joining the Navy would be a quick short-cut up the ladder to an officer's rank.

The college's technical head was Dai Rees. Dai had served on the *Mauritania*, sister ship to the *Lusitania* launched in 1906 by the Cunard Line. The *Mauritania* was the fastest passenger liner crossing the Atlantic at the time. The *Lusitania* was sunk by a German U-boat in 1915, with a loss of 1,118 passengers and crew off Kinsale Head in Cork in the South of Ireland.

At college we were taught to send and receive messages. We were given radio sets that had been assembled with deliberate faults, and taught to repair them. The college overlooked Caswell Bay, and although we were students, and the course administered by the Merchant Navy, we were allowed to wear uniforms and take part in parades on the beach below.

I then kicked my heels for a while, waiting for a ship. I then received my official call-up papers just before my eighteenth birthday. I could have chosen any arm of the services. I naturally chose the Royal Navy.

Meanwhile, I continued with my radio studies combining it with navigation, as I have previously noted. Later on in life I lectured for a number of years on navigation at the Education Centre at Pwll, emphasising the importance of being able to read charts and impart clear and precise directions over the radio. In an emergency it is imperative that any one in an emergency should report his or her position precisely and calmly. It is a matter of pride to me that one of

With Ardis Timmis on board the
Nautilus *submarine in Mystic, Connecticut*

my pupils managed recently to circumnavigate the globe in his sailing boat.

Because a part of my duties on the *Creole* during my time in the Royal Navy was to chase down German U-boats it was an interesting experience, years later in America, to board one of the world's most famous submarines. Dill and I had become friendly with Jim and Ardis Timmis in New York. Ardis took me along to Mystic, Connecticut, where the nuclear submarine lay at anchor. It was interesting to be able to see at close quarters the world's first submarine to travel beneath the North Pole. By the time I saw it, the sub had been decommissioned and was the main attraction at the National Submarine Museum.

The *Nautilus* was launched in 1954 by the wife of Dwight D Eisenhower and it was in service until 1979. Other submarine and ships were named *Nautilus*, including Captain Nemo's famous sub in *Twenty Thousand Leagues Under the Sea* and in *Mysterious Island*.

Another interesting incident was when I was invited through friends to sail with the Mayor of Albany, Mayor Toughy, on his yacht *The Content*, a single-masted forty-four foot vessel. We embarked from Salem, Marble Head round to Gloucester, Block Island and Rockfort. On the way we encountered a twister and had to batten the hatches and ride out the storm.

I bought my first boat in the early 1960s. It was a 7.5 metre cruiser, built of mahogany in Berlin as a police river boat. As such, it had been designed primarily for speed. I spotted it in Tenby where I had gone specifically to look for a suitable boat. And there it was, perched on a trailer. I fell in love with it at first sight. It was its shape that first attracted me, especially the shape of its bow. I realised it was in dire need of renovation. But I bought it anyway for £950 and towed it back to Pwll, where I was living by then, and parked it outside. And there I worked hard at it. I dismantled the engine completely bit by bit and rebuilt it. It was a petrol engine rather than diesel, which was a disadvantage as a petrol engine was more inflammable and more dangerous in an accident. At the time at the Centre I was lecturing on vehicle maintenance so I had some experience of working on engines. The woodwork and metalwork training I had received and had taught was also useful. In addition to the work being a necessity for renovating my boat, I found it pleasurable as well.

The boat had been built in the classical style consisting of wooden planks fixed in place with copper nails. It took me almost eighteen months to complete the renovation. I then sailed it to Burry Port. There I named it *Creole Bach*, after the name of the ship I had served on.

I was assisted in its launching by a German who was the manager of the Thyssen company at Bynea. On one arm he sported a swastika tattoo, a relic of his time in the Hitler Youth. We were forced to wait for the tide to come in, and then I steered it out to sea for the first time. It was a wonderful moment. We did not break a bottle of Champagne across its bow but my helper did drink a bottle of beer for luck.

The *Creole Bach* had two berths and I enjoyed sailing it over to Tenby, a voyage that took me six hours. I also visited Milford and Neyland. And it was at Milford that I anchored it for a while. I kept it for over ten years. And it was at Milford that I eventually sold it for £2,500 to a Cardiganshire businessman. It might seem like a good profit, but no, I had spent some considerable money on its

In the role of Commodore of Burry Port Sailing Club in 1988, welcoming the two women who replicated Amelia Earhart's sea-plane landing at Porth Tywyn

renovation and dedicated hundreds of working hours as a labour of love restoring it. In fact, I felt rather sad when I sold it.

My local interest in all things maritime was instrumental in my being elected Commodore of Burry Port Sailing Club in 1988. That year we celebrated the sixtieth anniversary of Amelia Earhart's historical landing in her sea-plane, an event referred to earlier. The occasion was re-enacted with two women landing their sea-plane on the same spot. I then sailed out to greet them and ferry them to the shore.

Amelia's dream had been to be the first woman to fly across the Atlantic Ocean. On 17 June 1928 she took off in her Fokker 7, *The Friendship*, together with two co-pilots, Wilmer Stultz and Louis Gordon. After a flight lasting 20 hours and 40 minutes they landed at Burry Port.

It must have been an amazing sight, the plane appearing through the clouds and landing on the water at Pwll. The first to row over to to find out what was happening was a local character, Dai Harvey, who was out fishing in his rowing boat, the *Black Pad*. He was given quite a shock. But over he went and opened the door. A load of empty beer bottles rolled out to meet him. As there was prohibition in America at the time, the crew must have made up for it on their way over. Then Dai heard a voice speaking with an American accent inquiring of their position. Dai answered, 'Second Slip Pwll!' As far as the flight crew could tell, he might as well have told them they had landed on the moon!

A great crowd gathered for the anniversary celebrations including the local Member of Parliament, Denzil Davies. We recreated the movements of the crew by visiting Frickers Café, where Amelia had enjoyed a cup of tea after her historic landing. Unfortunately the café has since been demolished.

Amelia disappeared while on another flight over the Far East. No remains were found of her or her plane. But at Burry Port a memorial stands in tribute to her great achievement and bravery.

Today, I am constantly reminded of Amelia's great feat. From my lounge window I can see the exact spot where she landed, and where, all those years ago, a dead whale was washed ashore.

The second boat I bought was a two-masted Fisher 30 with a canoe-style stern. This kind of craft takes the waves better than a boat such as the *Creole Bach*, especially in a following sea. My new boat had a Mercedes 36 engine.

I spotted this one at Benalmedina near Malaga in Spain when I was looking for a replacement for the *Creole Bach*. This one cost me £16,500. It needed a lot of work before I could sail it but I worked on it and it was sailed back to Neyland. There in the boatyard I kept it while I cleaned and painted it. Family members and friends often stayed on it. It was four-berthed and, should the need arise, one could sleep in the cabin. I named this *Creole Las* (the blue Creole).

The big difference between this one and *Creole Bach* was that this one sat on the water rather than in it. This meant it was slower. But it was fast enough for me to sail it on the Cleddau. There I had to be wary of the huge tankers that passed to and fro. Maritime rules insist, of course, that small boats have to give way to larger boats. And the tankers on the Cleddau did not offer much of an option.

In 1993 I sailed *Creole Las* all the way to Menorca. This meant sailing for Bordeaux and then following the river Gironde. During the days that took me as far as the Midi Canal, that connects the Atlantic to the Mediterranean, I had Neil's company and help. We decided to stay awhile in Agen. We entered the harbour there at too much speed and this resulted in a nasty scrape along the side of the boat. Agen has been twinned with Llanelli and like Llanelli it has a well-known rugby team. We spent the night there, and because of our civic connection, Neil was invited to deliver an address at the Town Hall.

We then left the boat there and returned home for a three-week break. Neil was unable to resume as crew because of his work, so Mervyn accompanied me. And that's when I took on board the most unlikely sailor since Noah. The Rev Elfed Lewys decided to come along with us. Elfed was an eccentric that was beyond eccentricity. With his booming voice, there was no need for a foghorn. And time meant absolutely nothing to him. To Elfed there was no difference whatever between two o' clock in the afternoon and two o' clock in the morning. I knew we were in for a pantomime.

Elfed wasn't used to sailing so he demanded that I should teach him to work ropes by practising on my front lawn. This entailed throwing ropes up into the pine trees, imagining they were masts. I there and then decided to appoint him head cook.

He had moved to the area as a minister, and he would often call to see me, usually during the early hours of the morning when he would chat about any and every subject under the sun. He had been known to fall asleep in his chair only to continue the conversation when he woke up. He would usually turn up with his pet pooch, '*Tês Fach yr Haf*' (little morning sunshine). He maintained that he had taught Tês to sing the Welsh National Anthem as well as 'Sospan Fach'. The latter was a must, as Elfed was a staunch Scarlets fan. Unfortunately, both tunes sounded exactly the same.

It is difficult to describe the experience of having Elfed on board. He was almost impossible to cope with on dry land. On board, he was an accident waiting to happen. The appropriate word that described Elfed was probably 'different'. But he was determined to come along, and he flew out with me. Mervyn arrived the next day. When he arrived, Elfed made himself clear. He was to be in charge. No-one would treat him as a lackey. But he did agree to be our chef, a word that was to be used loosely. On voyage he must have opened dozens of soup tins.

We sailed at a very slow rate, around 5 miles an hour. The boat was drawing around 5 feet of water below and we had to be very aware of boats coming to meet us. On the way to Toulouse we sailed through a vineyard, where we anchored overnight. The area is famous for its Pinot Noir. Elfed appeared on deck sprucely dressed and looking very tidy. He had even combed his hair. On a sudden whim he had decided to pay a visit to the vineyard owner, although he had no idea who the owner might be or where he lived. Off he went. It was morning when he returned, and when he finally appeared he was clutching as many bottles of wine as he could carry. He had been pontificating, he said, with the vineyard owner, who couldn't speak a word of English. And Elfed spoke not one word of French. But there had been no problem, according to Elfed. The owner had spoken in French while Elfed spoke Welsh.

As we progressed along the canal we heard a shout from the bank one day. Someone was asking, in French, if we had happened to see a car? We felt a bump, and we realised that we had hit a car that was submerged in the canal. It must have been a green car, as we later found traces of green paint on the hull. We must have been the only crew in history to collide with a car in a canal.

At Toulouse it was time to change crew, so we headed for home. Little did I realise at the time that Elfed would not be long with us. He died suddenly at his sister's home at Pontypridd on 12 February 1999. The memorial service, held at Nazareth Chapel, Pont-iets, was more like a thanksgiving service. There were many more smiles there than tears. Elfed would have loved that. He made everyone he met feel better.

I spent a month at home before resuming the voyage. With me there were two new crews, Nick Carter, an ex-Naval man like me, and Richard Thorpe, another friend. Off we sailed towards the Narbonne, and there we experienced an unexpected event. We heard gunshots, and there on the bank were a crowd of feuding gipsies. We went past at full speed.

Later, seeing that the fuel tanks were low, Richard and I went ahead to buy diesel. When we returned, the boat was besieged by a horde of rats on the jetty. They were scurrying around and were in danger of boarding the boat. Nick was a crack shot and had competed at Bisley, but unfortunately he had not brought his gun along with him ... We hastily battened down the hatches; otherwise we would have left with some very unwelcome guests.

We reached the Mediterranean and sailed for the next few days towards Rosas on the Spanish Costa Brava. There on the mainland we stayed for a while preparing for our final leg to Menorca. There we removed the planks and old tyres we had fixed around the boat to protect it from any damage that could have been caused by the canal banks.

We decided to enjoy some luxury, so rather than spending the night on the boat I decided to look for on-shore accommodation. So I tied up at a convenient berth. When I returned I discovered that I had tied up at the Commodore's berth. This was not wise, so I soon moved. The next morning we upped anchor, and having listened to the weather forecast in case of an impending storm, we set sail for the northern coast of Menorca.

We headed for the small fishing village of Fornells that stands on a small bay and near a beautiful harbour. The village was first established as a refuge for pirates during the eighteenth century. The harbour has only a narrow entrance, making the bay practically a lake. The little houses painted white, blue and ochre offer a picture-postcard scene. We made land as the morning sun was rising over the lighthouse. It was a magical sight.

The whole voyage, including breaks at home, took around three months all told. I seriously considered mooring the boat permanently at Fornells, but unfortunately, beautiful as the place is, it remains open to the strong winter winds. It would have been fine in summer, but I had a problem finding a suitable winter berth. And so, after a night's rest, we weighed anchor and set off for Port d'Addaya on the north-eastern coast. And I berthed it there for a year. It is a place much frequented by divers and surfers but it is also ideal for people like me who love to do nothing more energetic than idling and taking the occasional swim.

When the year was up, and the boat needed some maintenance work, I decided to take it home. I sailed as far as Barcelona and then towed it back home on a trailer. I worked on it for a time at Neyland and then I sold it to an undertaker. I felt quite lost without it, but the offer made by the undertaker was too good to refuse.

I had fallen in love with the Mediterranean and I desperately needed another boat. I had liked Menorca and had made quite a few friends there. Indeed, I had joined a band at Port d'Addaya in the Club San Clemente, where we performed every Thursday night.

Then in 2001 I visited Port de Pollenca on the northern coast of Mallorca, a town that boasts a huge marina and sailing club. I was eager to visit Mallorca because of the island's connections with Chopin, one of my favourite composers. He spent a few years in Valldemossa with the writer George Sand, and his piano can still be seen in a museum in the town.

At the marina at Port de Pollenca I happened to meet the owner of one of the boats that were moored there. It was for sale. It was an old boat, berthed at Jetty 4. It made a sad sight. Its paint was peeling and it was obviously in need of a refit. It had no tools or equipment save for one hammer, used as a prop placed upside down to secure the ventilation switch in place. But I immediately realised that the boat held a definite potential. And so I struck a bargain with the owner and became the new owner of the *Talahaut*. I intend to change the name to either *Creole 4* or *Creoleto*, thus continuing the tradition.

The *Talahaut* is a forty-foot sailing trawler with a double screw and two 120 horse power diesel engines. It can reach a speed of 15 land miles an hour. It is the best boat I have ever owned, primarily because of the space it offers. It was built in Taiwan and fashioned from teak.

Performing with Santiago Bo and friends in Cala Rajata, Mallorca

*Santiago Bo and me performing in the Fat Cat Jazz Club
in Port de Pollenca, Mallorca*

Since buying the *Talahaut* I have visited Port dè Pollenca at least
four times a year, sleeping on board. There are six berths – two
singles up front and a double bed aft, and should the need arise, two
can sleep in the galley. With regular flights from Cardiff Airport to
Palma, a flight of just over two hours, and a 40-minute drive to Port
de Pollenca by car or bus, it is an easy trip to make.

Just a few miles west of the port lies the old town of Pollenca with
its ancient buildings and open-air market. It possesses an ancient
ambience and seems as if it hasn't changed over the centuries. It is a
town worth visiting if only to see Calvary, where 365 steps lead past
a row of stone crosses up to the church on the hill.

I enjoy visiting Pollenca for the occasional meal and a glass of
wine. I have made numerous friends in the area and on Sundays, in
the port, I perform with a local band at the El Ancla restaurant. El
Ancla is Catalan for 'the anchor'. The other members of the band are
Catcho on tenor sax, Louis on the drums, Guiliamo on guitar and
Santiago Bo on the alto saxophone. They are all Catalans.

It all started when I happened to visit El Ancla one Sunday and
heard the band playing 'Since My Best Gal Turned Me Down', one
of Bix Beiderbeck's masterpieces. I chatted to Santiago, and the next
Sunday I was performing with the band. We played some of the
classics, among them 'Jazz Me Blues' and 'Royal Garden Blues', 'All

of Me' and 'Satin Doll'. As well as appearing with the band I also play in a duet with Guiliamo. Another venue where I often appear on the island is the Diving Club at Cala Rajata, to the south east of Porta de Pollenca.

Music to me is an international language that needs no words, one that crosses boundaries and binds people together. And it is a means of making friends. One night at El Ancla, Rosemary and I met Dafydd and Val from Cricieth. They often go over when we do. Dafydd and I enjoy swimming while Rosemary and Val share the same interest, needlework. Indeed, we tend to meet many Welsh people at Port de Pollenca. Both the Red Dragon and the Glyndŵr flag fly from the mast of the *Talahaut* and I am often greeted in Welsh from the jetty by people who spot them.

Thanks to the Harlem Blues and Jazz band I visited the States extensively. Although based in New York, I managed to travel north up to Chicago, the Great Lakes and Niagara Falls and across the border to Montreal and Toronto. In New York State I visited one of the Seneca Indians Reservation. Seneca means 'The Mountain People'. Other places of interest I visited included Baltimore, the Wright Brothers' Museum, the Naval Base at Norfolk Virginia and the site at Cape Cod from where Marconi sent his first radio message across the Atlantic to Lavernock Point near Penarth. At Saratoga Performing Arts Centre I was fortunate enough to meet Benny Goodman, Gene Krupa and Teddy Wilson.

Playing with the band led to many European visits. Among other venues we appeared at the Ghent Jazz Festival. In Belgium at Mechelen I met Rene Savels, who became a close friend. The only instrument Rene played was the washboard! But he was a great jazz aficionado and an excellent artist. Many of his paintings grace the walls of my lounge.

I have visited the West Indies as well on various occasions. Usually we would perform in New York before flying up to Boston and on to Miami and on again to Nassau. We would stay at Ocean Spray, a very opulent place by the harbour where liners and yachts from all parts of the world stop over. I played with a band there too, a group of musicians from Cuba.

Once I happened to meet a man from Crewe who performed with a ship's band. He invited me aboard for supper and I later joined the band as part of the entertainment organised for the passengers. This sort of thing happens often.

Unfortunately, racism can raise its ugly head even in the most idyllic of places. I once met a man there who was a banker. He and his wife were members of the sailing club at Nassau. I was invited to join them for dinner where I met a very friendly local. I mentioned to my two friends how nice he was. 'Oh, we don't socialise with him,' said the banker's wife. 'He applied to be Commodore of our Sailing Club and he even made it to the short list. Luckily, however, we discovered just in time that he was marked with the tar brush.' Yes, racism is alive and still raises its ugly head. It really makes my blood boil. Imagine the woman condemning a man for having black genes in his blood when he, unlike her, was living and working in his own country.

I was involved in a most unexpected incident on another occasion, in Barbados this time. Rosemary was sunbathing on the beach while I was swimming, when two lads approached her and asked for a cigarette. She obliged, and they sat down to talk. I came out of the water and joined them. We shared a few bottles of beer and they invited us to a barbeque in the garden of their rented house. They played karaoke music and surprised us by including Welsh Christmas carols.

When they realised that I played clarinet, one of the lads said that his father had played tenor sax in Norway. In fact, he had backed Ella Fitzgerald. He and Ella became lovers, and Ella would sometimes sing the lad to sleep. I later realised that his father was the famous Norwegian saxophonist Thor Einar Larsen. There had been a rumour that he and Ella had been secretly married.

I have often, while on cruises, been invited to perform with various ships' bands. But my favourite destinations are Mallorca and Menorca. I like the Spanish people. They are never rushed and make time to be welcoming and sociable. I have tried to learn enough of the language to enable me to get by. I am anything but fluent, but my sister Margery speaks perfect Spanish. She spends half the year in Benalmedina near Malaga in Spain and the other half at home in New Quay. Her husband, Malcolm, was once Commodore of the New Quay Sailing Club, the very same club that brought Dill Jones and I together.

Between the music and the sea, and the combination of both I am a contented man. Waves and rhythms, they go hand in hand. And both are magical.

On board the Talahaut *in the Port de Pollenca marina, Mallorca*

Chapter 6

I worked as Warden of the Further Education Centre at Pwll until 1979. I was also in charge of its arts school. One regular visitor was Ray Gravell, the Llanelli and Wales rugby player. Every time we would meet, Ray would greet me with the question, 'Who is Peanuts Hucko?' He had heard that Glenn Miller's clarinettist was called Peanuts Hucko, and he loved the name. But he could never remember who he played with. Whenever we met, even on radio or television programmes, he would always ask me about Peanuts Hucko.

Gradually, I became Peanuts Hucko to Grav. Often, he would drive by in his car and he would always wind the window down and shout, 'Peanuts Hucko!' If he met me on the street, I would be referred to as Peanuts Hucko. He just loved the name. In fact I had met Peanuts Hucko together with Earl 'Fatha' Hines and Jack Teagarden at the Maendy in Cardiff when I was a youth.

Llanelli without Grav is a very empty and quiet place. He was always around, and I would invariably hear him well before I'd see him. I never met anyone with so many interests. He could talk the hind leg off a donkey on any subject on earth. He had a huge soul, a huge heart and was a big man in every way. That was Grav. The truest Welshman I ever met. He can be heard singing *'Sospan Fach'* with the band on my CD, *Wyn a'i Fyd*.

The Centre became quite an attraction, both educational and recreational. There was a stage and a piano, two necessities for making it a music venue. And then something very important happened to me. In 1975, four years before I retired, I married again. I had been a single man for over a quarter of a century and during all that time I had only been involved in one serious affair. Despite the huge success of the Centre I was going through a difficult patch. I was feeling low and was on medication. Then, when I was appearing one night in a hotel at Brecon organised by the Brecon Jazz Club I noticed a girl dressed in red in the audience. This was sometime in May. We chatted after the show and gradually we became an item. We married before the turn of the year.

Rosemary is from Llanfyllin and she worked as a teacher in

Rosemary in the garden of Y Pinwydd, between Pwll and Porth Tywyn

religious studies and games at Ysgol Gwernyfed in Brecon. As I was appearing regularly – about once a month – at the Brecon Jazz Club we would meet pretty regularly. We arranged to meet one Sunday at Builth Wells and then proceed to Brecon to meet her sister. I travelled over by train and she arrived in her new blue car. After tea at her sister's place we decided to drive up north to Froncysyllte. On the way we parked at a beauty spot above a picturesque valley. Before we left the car I persuaded Rosemary to move the car closer to the edge.

We wandered down the slope towards the river bank. I happened to look up towards the road and I saw the car creeping forward towards the edge. There was nothing we could do to stop it. We just watched it creep forward closer and closer to the edge before toppling over and landing below on its nose. We had to beg a local farmer to tow the car back onto the road with his tractor. Its front was flattened. I didn't know what to say. After all, it was my fault because I was the one who had told her to park nearer the edge. So there and then I asked her to marry me. She accepted. I think it was from pity more than anything else. How we reached Brecon, I'll never know. Rosemary's new blue car was a wreck.

Rosemary was keen on getting married on Boxing Day. But that is the day when Llanelli traditionally play Swansea in a rugby local derby. Boxing Day was therefore out of the question. So we decided to marry on the day after. The wedding was at Brecon and Terry James, my cousin, was the organist. Back then, Rosemary was a Welsh learner and the minister, as he recited the wedding vows was reading rather fast. So I slowly repeated the minister's words and Rosemary, in turn, repeated them to me.

I lived in a bungalow near the Education Centre at Pwll, next

Celebrating my marriage to Rosemary in Brecon in 1976

door to Mervyn. And we settled there. Then, in 1976 we moved to our present home, 'Y Pinwydd' (the pines) high above Pwll and Burry Port. To someone like me who loves the sea, it is perfectly located with the confluence of three rivers spread out below. From the front windows I can view a panorama of sea across to the Gower. We worked hard on the place over the years, and as both of us are quite handy in the various crafts, we did all the work ourselves.

By 1979 I had reached a crossroads in my career. I kept asking myself whether I should retire or not. I had a choice, to continue for another three years until I reached retiring age or take early retirement. I weighed up the pros and cons. Practically every day I would see Alwyn and Mervyn, both of them retired, driving past on their way to play golf at Ashburnham. How I envied them their freedom. Mervyn had been a teacher and had taken early retirement. Alwyn had also been a teacher specialising in child psychology. My work still gave me much pleasure, but seeing them enjoying themselves so much, I decided to join them in retirement.

It was a difficult step to take. Yes, my musical career with the band was still thriving, with regular calls for us to perform. But could I live on that alone? The only way I could answer the question was to

With presenter Vaughan Hughes on the set of Y Byd yn ei Le

hand in my notice. Just over a month later I got a lucky break. HTV was contracted to produce a live weekly discussion programme, *Y Byd yn ei Le* (The World in its Place). In addition to debating current affairs there was a weekly musical slot involving a topical song reflecting the events of the week. The programme was to be presented by Vaughan Hughes and I was asked to provide the music with my band. There would be various vocalists, mainly Gary Owen and Dyfed Thomas as well as Ray Gravell and Heather Jones. I jumped at the chance. I composed a signature tune to open and close the show.

A controversial subject would be chosen every week and a panel reflecting varying opinions invited to the studio. When I was given the particular chosen subject I would contact either Dic Jones or John Gwilym Jones, and one or the other would compose topical verses on the subject. I would then arrange the words to be sung to a popular tune. Sometimes a late story would break and everything would have to be changed at short notice. Somehow or other, I never missed the deadline.

Being a live programme, it presented quite a risk. On one occasion the Porta-prompt, a device fixed to the front of a camera and listing the words, broke down. Gary Owen was the vocalist that night and to his credit he carried on to the end of the song like a true trouper without a hitch.

Members of the band at this time were Brian Breeze, guitar; Peter Lewis, drums; John Phillips, piano; Wyn Davies, bass; Mervyn, my brother, on vibes, and myself on clarinet. The show ran on HTV for three years.

More work came along, not all of it musical. I worked in Welsh-language drama series like *Heliwr, Mwy Na Phapur Newydd* and *Dihirod Dyfed*. Among the various characters I played, I portrayed the father of executed murderer Ronnie Harries, the man I had often

The band formed in 1979 for the television programme Y Byd yn ei Le:
John Phillips (piano), Wyn Davies (bass), Brian Breeze (guitar), me,
Peter Lewis (drums) and my brother Mervyn (vibes)

seen driving around in his Land Rover when I taught at Laugharne.

In the same production, my brother Mervyn played the role of a vicar. One day we were all dressed up for our parts and on our way to the shoot in a bus. A delivery man had blocked the road with his van and wouldn't move. Mervyn left the bus and gave him a mouthful of abuse followed by a V-sign. The man was so shocked that he moved immediately.

Meanwhile, the gigs continued. As well as calls to perform all over Wales there were more regular appearances. Between 1994 and 1999 the band performed regularly at the Milford Haven Jazz Club in the Lord Nelson. I was billed in a headline in the Mercury, the local paper as 'The Man who puts the Jazz in Milford'. I would travel on Mondays and stay overnight. The line-up was Bobby Main, tenor sax and trumpet, Billy Jenkins, piano, Nick Carter, bass, Derek Adams, trombone, Paul Warrington, trumpet, Ned Rolls, drums and myself on vibes and clarinet. We performed songs like 'Satin Doll', 'I Can't Give You Anything But Love', 'Tin Roof Blues', and 'Lonesome Road'. During the day we held sessions for schoolkids. At

Appearing in the S4C programme Cwpwrdd Dillad
in 2007, with Sioned Geraint and Nia Parry

A jazz course in Ferryside, 2005

the end of the school course the school jazz band performed 'C-Jam Blues'.

I began lecturing on the history of jazz, and then I led a project named The Jazz Train, a weekly excursion from Carmarthen to Milford Haven. This involved the band performing on the train every Monday. The band also recorded a two-hour documentary directed by Meredydd Evans on jazz in religion. Our vocalist was Ann Burrows, who also sings on two tracks on the CD *Wyn a'i Fyd*. Ann's voice was perfect for religious songs.

Meanwhile, the foreign trips continued. Religious history tells us that three pilgrimages to St David's equalled one pilgrimage to Rome. In jazz, it would be true to say that New Orleans is the equal of what Rome was to Christians in the Age of the Saints. I have visited New Orleans three times. This must mean that I have secured my ticket to the musical gods' top table in jazz heaven.

My first visit coincided with a visit to New York to see Dill. I flew from La Guardia down to New Orleans. I had considered going by train, but that would have taken the best part of two days. Dill had briefed me on the places I should visit as well as providing me with names of interesting people I should try to meet. High on the list of

In New York, with the famous Twin Towers in the background,
towers that are not there now...

priorities was a voyage on the *Natchez*, the famous paddle steamboat that sails along the Mississippi.

Of course, one venue I wouldn't dare miss was Preservation Hall, the city's jazz temple where I saw, amongst others, Willie Humphrey on clarinet. He had been a member of King Oliver's band. I was surprised at how small the place was, not unlike Mam-gu's house back in Marble Hall Road. It was as if two rooms had been knocked into one. Above the entrance were suspended a trombone case and a clarinet case. Another surprise was the fact that the musicians played at a comparatively low volume.

I stayed in a hotel in Charles Street, and Hywel Gwynfryn, presenter of the early morning Welsh radio programme 'Helo Bobol' on Radio Cymru, had arranged to interview me live over the phone. Unfortunately, it was to be transmitted at an unearthly hour because of the time difference. While awaiting the call I spent the time in the swimming pool, the only way I could stay awake.

On my second visit, my son Neil came with me. We stayed at La Pavilione, a small but attractive hotel. Naturally, I took Neil along to Preservation Hall. This time there was a notice pinned on the wall stating, 'The Saints, five dollars. Others, one dollar.' The band was so fed up with requests for 'When the Saints Go Marching In' that they charged more for playing it!

I had intended taking Neil aboard the *Natchez* for a trip along the river. We were late arriving and it had left. We were lucky. On her way out she collided with another boat and some thirty passengers were hurt. Then a thunderstorm broke and we arrived back at the hotel soaked to the skin. On the television a warning was posted warning everyone to stay indoors because alligators were swimming in the sidewalk gutters!

My third visit was in 2008, and again Neil came along with me. This time we stayed in a hotel in Canal Street, the city's main thoroughfare in the French Quarter, or Vieux Carre. The Harlem Blues and Jazz band were there and we performed at the Heritage Festival. This time we flew from Cardiff Airport to Amsterdam, on to Detroit and on again to New Orleans.

The effects of Hurricane Katrina three years previously were still evident. People still lived in caravans, in tents and under bridges. I felt very guilty. There I was staying in a posh hotel while all around there were hundreds of people without a permanent roof over their heads, and without even clean water. Following the hurricane, some 80 per cent of the city was under water and 18,000 people died. The effects of the hurricane caused damage amounting to $81 billion, the costliest disaster ever. I couldn't believe the fact that President Bush had not deemed it necessary to visit the city. He merely flew over the city in his helicopter.

Life, however, went on. In one restaurant a band was playing Thirties music. The atmosphere of the era was recreated by women dancing and waving handkerchiefs and parasols. Playing alto sax was Sammy Rimmington. During the break I approached him and told him that I knew he was sixty-eight years old. He was amazed, and asked me how I knew. I told him I remembered seeing him perform at the Ritz in Llanelli in 1956, when he was a sixteen-year-old youth playing with Ken Colyer's band. He couldn't believe it.

From New Orleans we decided to fly over to Nassau in the Bahamas. On our drive to the airport, the taxi driver took us on a detour to show us where soul and gospel singer Mahalia Jackson had been buried, placed in a glass coffin. We stopped, and there by the cemetery was an arms shop selling guns and ammunition of every kind. How ironic, I thought. Murderous arms were being sold next to the grave of a singer who had promoted peace and love.

I have more than once found how true that old adage of the world being a small place can be. At the airport in Miami I started chatting to a complete stranger. He told me he lived on Paradise Island. I told him that a cousin of mine lived there. I was stunned when he told me he knew Terry James well, he and Richard Harris who shared his house. The house had been completely washed away during a tropical storm. Nothing remained of the house. The man invited us to stay at his home whenever we wished.

All my visits to America were to the east coast save for one. I did once fly from La Guardia to Los Angeles and travelled on to San Francisco. I then visited a place called Cambrai, where Welsh immigrants had once settled. I performed there with a local band. Among my American visits, one of the highlights was the visit to New York in 1993 with a television crew from the Welsh series *Hel Straeon*. It coincided with my annual visit to play with the Harlem

Blues and Jazz Band, an event that has, since 1984, turned into a pilgrimage to Dill Jones' old haunts. We stayed at the Omni Park Hotel near Central Park, across the road from Carnegie Hall, where many jazz legends have appeared over the years. We visited Al Vollmer's home at Larchmont, Al being the band's manager, where we rehearsed. We were filmed performing in venues such as The Red Blazer in Midtown West Manhattan, the Cat Club on Broadway and at Sweet Basil in Greenwich Village. At the Cat Club I was privileged to meet on stage the trumpeter and vocalist Doc Cheetham, who was well into his nineties.

Another venue where I was filmed during a performance was the Right Bank Cafe under Williamsburgh Bridge with trumpeter Mike Lattimore, drummer Wes Landers and, of course, Johnny Williams on bass. The event was a tribute to the legendary pianist Shorty Jackson, who had died a fortnight previously. He worked as an undertaker. As his nickname suggests, he was little taller than four feet, but on piano he was a genius.

The documentary was named *Pump Hewl i Harlem* (Five Roads to Harlem). The programme opened with me and the band playing a gig at Five Roads near Llanelli. We then flew to New York, visiting

With Bubba Brooks in the Louisiana Club on Broadway,
New York, in the 1990s

With Johnny Williams, former bassist with Louis Armstrong, in Harlem

Harlem, the cradle of New York jazz. Johnny Williams showed us around Harlem, where he lived at Sugar Hill. At one time the area was the richest in the city. He showed us musical venues such as the Apollo, the Cotton Club, the Savoy, the Lafayette, and Small's Paradise. During Johnny's early days, no black performer was allowed to use the same door as white musicians. Today, only the Apollo remains.

Up until 1873, Harlem was a village that stood apart from New York. It was first colonised by the Dutch, who stole the land from the native Americans, the Lenape. Continued immigration made it a cosmopolitan crucible with ghettos formed by Jews, Italians, Spaniards, Irish and, of course, Afro-Caribbean. The blacks began arriving around 1900, and by the middle of the last century it had become America's black capital.

Harlem witnessed highs and lows. It was the centre of culture before the Depression and the Second World War led to unemployment, transforming it into the city's criminal centre with the attendant hopelessness and despair. Johnny, however, did not express any bitterness as he showed us around. He showed us where the Tree of Hope once stood between the Lafayette Theatre and

Connie's Inn. Performers such as Ethel Waters, Fletcher Henderson and Ubie Blake would caress the elm tree. Johnny and other black musicians would do likewise according to the old tradition that to do so would bring luck. It was a futile hope, of course. The tree was cut down in 1934, but a piece of it is still preserved at the Apollo.

Jazz, in the meantime, moved nearby to Greenwich Village particularly, an area of bars and cafes where many young people hang around. This was the area where revolution was preached and sung in the early sixties by protest singers such as Bob Dylan and Joan Baez. With the New York University located in the area, the vivacity still remains. Nearby also stands the White Horse Tavern, Dylan Thomas' favourite New York bar.

Changes in jazz, both in location and in style, are not a wholly bad thing. There is a need for a transfusion of new blood occasionally. But some changes are sadder than others. By the beginning of the 1990s, some of the stars of the Harlem Blues and Jazz Band had died and been replaced. For instance, the trumpeter in 1993 was Bill Dillard. He was in his eighties and could remember his time with jazz legends Jelly Roll Morton and King Oliver. I would arrive every year to find someone missing and a new face in the band. I often wonder where and how Al Vollmer keeps finding the old stars.

Then, in 1998 I was back and being filmed by Agenda at my old friend Johnny Williams' memorial service. Johnny was one of the nicest people on God's earth. Four years earlier, HTV had surprised me with a birthday celebration when I was sixty-five years old. The highlight of the evening at the hall in Burry Port was the unexpected arrival of the band, with Johnny among them. It was a very emotional moment.

I had no idea that such a celebration was being planned by HTV. The presenter, Arfon Haines Davies, fooled me completely. Rosemary had known about it for weeks and had been under great pressure trying to keep me from discovering the secret.

The media has been very good to me. I presented a jazz series on the television magazine programme *Wedi 3*, as well as a series twice a week on Swansea Sound. I have also presented series on jazz on Radio Wales and Radio Cymru. It has always been a pleasure to be invited to talk about a subject that has been close to my heart for over

The night of the Penblwydd Hapus *show, with the Harlem Blues and Jazz Band:*
Bill Nichols, Al Casey, Johnny Williams, Al Vollmer, Freddie Smith and
Bubba Brooke

seventy years. When I was head of the Further Education Centre at
Pwll I wrote a book on the history and development of wind
instruments, with special reference to the clarinet. And recently, the
Welsh Assembly Government's Education Department produced
seven thousand CDs of the band and I performing a Welsh folk tune.
The discs have been distributed around schools in Wales.

One event that I am proud to have been involved with is Brecon
Jazz. I have been associated with it from the very beginning when its
forerunner, the Welsh Jazz Festival, was held at the Chapter Theatre,
Cardiff in 1983, before it moved the following year to Brecon. In that
first venture at Cardiff my band performed and I also appeared with
Dill and with Humphrey Lyttelton.

Humph once played my version of Duke Ellington's 'Black
Butterfly' on his radio programme and posed two questions for the
listeners – who was the clarinettist? And what nationality was he? He
was kind enough to pay me a few compliments. He liked Wales as he
had lived for a while at Felindre when he worked at the Port Talbot
steel works. He had heard Welsh songs being sung at the works'
social club and in the pubs.

The last time I performed with him was at the Market Hall in
2007 at Brecon Jazz. As we said our goodbyes I told I would see him

at the festival the following year. He assured me he would be there. Sadly, he died in April the following year. He was a great musician and a gentleman.

Many of the jazz greats have appeared at Brecon, among them Lionel Hampton, Clark Terry, Slim Gaillard, George Melly, Slam Stewart, Scott Hamilton, Bruce Turner, George James, who had been a member of Louis Armstrong's band, Jay McShann, the Kansas City Pianist, and the Harlem Blues and Jazz Band, of course. One year I remember bumping into Meic Stevens, the singer-songwriter from Solva, in the crowd. I invited him on stage to perform a few blues. I felt bad that Meic had not been invited officially to perform there. He began his career playing jazz as a banjo player with Mike Harries' band in Cardiff. Meic is a great blues performer, up there with the best. I tend to jump at any opportunity of appearing with Meic.

An ever-present performer at Brecon Jazz was George Melly. George joined my band as a guest at Cwmbran once. He arrived on his motorbike wearing a bright yellow helmet and balancing a box containing six bottles of wine on the tank. He had decided to learn Welsh. On stage that night he attempted to say a few words of Welsh,

Performing with Meic Stevens, the songsmith from Solva, in Brecon Jazz

but soon gave up. He blamed the wine.

There was just a curtailed Brecon Jazz in 2009, but plans have been announced for a festival in 2010. The organisers can have a new beginning. It can herald a significant step forward. There are more and more young Welsh musicians emerging, such as harpist Catrin Finch, pianist Iwan Llywelyn Jones and clarinettist Rhys Taylor playing more contemporary music. I believe this is an exciting period with more and more young people making the scene.

Every generation brings new elements into jazz. When I was young, classical jazz was in vogue, music played by Ellington, Basie and Armstrong. And Harry James as well, a Welshman, by the way. I once met him. His family lived in Tin Street in Cardiff before they emigrated to America at the time of the Great War. His father was a circus performer, as was Harry initially. He went on to marry actress Betty Grable and became one of the jazz greats.

They are all long gone and others have taken their place. You can't remain in the past. There is a place for all kinds of styles in jazz, including electronic music even though it tends to lack soul and seems to be rather mechanical. But I welcome new elements. The story of traditional, classical jazz is the story of an era, and that era has passed. And at Brecon, now is the time to begin again with a blank page.

Deian Hopkin is a prime example of my philosophy. When he was a boy at Llanelli, his mother would bring him along to see us play at places like Lampeter, and even further afield. He developed into a fine pianist, developing a totally different style to our traditional swing. He turned to modern at the Inter-college Eisteddfod at Aberystwyth when Russ Jones and I were adjudicating. We awarded him first prize as the best instrumentalist.

He went on to form his own band, 'Neges', and played at Brecon. I also remember Deian on a particularly sad night in 1979. He was appearing with us at the Marine Hotel in Aberystwyth and the result of the Referendum on a Welsh Assembly had just been announced. That night, both of us had the right to sing the blues.

But what is jazz? That is a question that I am continually asked. And it is a very difficult question to answer. It is like asking what love is. It is like asking me to describe birdsong. Every bird has its own song, its own voice. Every nation on earth has songs that can be

With Deian Hopkin's band 'Neges' in Brecon Jazz

described as jazz. Here in Wales, standards such as *'Tra Bo Dau'* and *'Dafydd y Garreg Wen'* can easily be adapted to a jazz style. The way to do so is to retain the composition but to change the accent and develop the melody. And discipline is paramount.

I remember a bass player I had once, Hubert Hughes, telling me excitedly on the way to a gig at the Ivy Bush in Carmarthen, 'Wyn, at last I know what jazz is. It is brain telepathy!' And he wasn't far from the truth. It all comes down to feeling, and expressing that feeling. Basically, it is a fusion of Afro-American music. Rhythm is central to it. Stir in some gospel and blues, music born of the slave trade, of exile, of mistreatment and killing, of endless toil in the cotton fields.

The central role that many Welsh people played in the slave trade grieves my heart. Many slaves were forced to adopt the surnames of their masters. The fact that so many black people adopted Welsh surnames speaks volumes. This is reflected in the surnames of numerous black jazz musicians. Take the surname Williams alone. You have Johnny Williams, the composers Clarence and Spencer Williams, Frank Williams, Bobby Williams, Cootie Williams and Mary Lou Williams, and many, many more. Then you have Miles Davis and Eddie 'Lockjaw' Davis. Add to them Quincy Jones, George Lewis and George James, and guitarist Calvin Edwards. You also have Earl 'Bud' Powell. And Kid Thomas, although his original surname was Valentine.

There is a distinct difference between black performers' interpretation of what we call 'hwyl' and the blues, and the white musician's interpretation. This was the mystic ingredient that Dill was searching throughout his life. Rhythm is an integral part of the black musician's make-up. It is as natural to them as breathing. White musicians have attempted to adopt black style and interpretation. Chicago was divided on musical lines. White music was performed in the North Side while black music was performed in the South Side. White musicians like Artie Shaw would visit the South Side specifically to listen to black music and to learn from it.

Black musicians had a slogan, 'I gotta right to sing the blues'. Louis performed a song based on it, 'I gotta right to sing the blues, I've gotta right to feel low down.' He did – the inheritance of decades of slavery and ill-treatment. Hearing white musicians trying to play black music to me is like hearing hymns being sung in church rather than in chapel. The 'hwyl' is missing.

Primarily, jazz isn't something to talk or to write about. Jazz is a feeling. When I flew out with a film crew to Johnny Williams' memorial service in 1998 the presenter, Angharad Mair – to her credit – tried to read up on the history of jazz. A book can be informative: it can explain various styles and outline details of developments and musicians. But it can't make you feel the music, live the music. It can't make you understand jazz because jazz is not of the mind but rather of the heart. Fats Waller summed it up perfectly when a certain lady approached him and asked, 'Tell me, Mr Waller, what is this thing they call jazz?' Fats answered, 'Madam, if you gotta ask, I guess you'll never know.' Some attribute the quote to Louis. But who said it isn't important. It was the perfect answer. Fats also said, 'If you don't know what it is, don't mess with it.' That is also true.

If you want to play jazz you have to learn chords, learn harmonies and, primarily, learn to listen. You can have brilliant musicians who can read notes on a copy as easy as reading through the alphabet. But there is a danger of sticking to – of being confined by – the copy. There are some who stick so meticulously to the written notes that should a fly land on the copy, they would play that as well. To me, the ear is more important than the eye. But above all, without feeling there is nothing. The heart is mightier than the head.

Despite the fact that there is freedom for variety within the tune, there is a recognised pattern to traditional jazz. The band in its entirety will open by playing the tune, the trumpeter playing the melody and the clarinet playing the harmony, the trombone providing the bass sound. The string instruments back up to provide the chords while the drums keep rhythm. Within the pattern, all the instrumentalists, in turn, play a solo while improvising the tune impromptu. Then the whole band will close with the original tune.

Modernists like Charlie Parker decided to break the old shackles and demanded more freedom, including freedom of expression. This became the music of the beats and the hipsters, mainly young whites who wanted to imitate black tastes. Often it would go hand in hand with modern poetry and art. It found a home among young intellectuals and young college students. It is all a matter of taste. To me, there is something missing from such music. The instrumentalists are – and were – masterly. But I don't get the feeling of communication that I get from traditional jazz. This communication should be twofold, not only between the instrumentalists but also between the band and the audience. I once discussed this with Humphrey Lyttleton. He also believed that the communication should involve the band elevating the audience and the audience's reaction, in turn, sharpening the response of the band. I do not believe that this is true of modern jazz. I believe it to be pretentious rubbish.

Jazz at its roots is a manifestation of the suffering of the black people. There is the sadness of the blues and the hope in the 'hwyl', or verve. In 1939, a mere seventy years ago, a Jewish musician, Abel Meeropol, composed a song called 'Strange Fruit'. It was sung by Billie Holiday, a black singer. The opening verse goes:

> Southern trees bear strange fruit
> Blood on the leaves and blood on the root,
> Black bodies swinging in the southern breeze,
> Strange fruit hanging from the poplar trees.

Yes, the strange fruit hanging from the branches of the poplar trees were corpses of black people. And when Billie Holiday performed in front of a white audience she was not allowed to move on stage. She, like all black women vocalists had to stand still as they sang. They were not allowed to enter or exit a theatre through the same doors as the white patrons. They would not be allowed to use the same stage door as white musicians: Billie Holiday and other black musicians were allowed to enter and to exit only through the service door.

I remember reading a social document published by the American government in 1937. It was the result of a study into the social standing of black American soldiers. They were described as strong, happy and faithful when properly fed. They were said to love music and possessed a sense of rhythm. They tended to be religiously inclined. And should they be properly managed, they would prove to be industrious. Among their negative traits there was a tendency for them to be garrulous and stubborn should they be treated badly. They were also liars and were immoral.

Imagine an official study coming to such a conclusion regarding fellow men. They were regarded not as people but as objects. The study was implemented. In the American army, blacks were used as drivers and mechanics. They were not placed in positions of authority. I saw this myself in Llanelli during the war.

Imagine Montgomery, Alabama in 1955 – a mere fifty-four years ago. Black people were expected to relinquish their seats on to white people on crowded buses. On a historical occasion, a seamstress, Rosa Parks, refused to do so. She was taken to court and fined one dollar and was ordered to pay four dollars in costs. But Rosa Parks' action that day reverberated all around the world.

The following year saw the release of the film *High Society* with Frank Sinatra, Bing Crosby, Grace Kelly and Louis Armstrong. When Crosby organised parties for his co-stars and the film crew, Armstrong, despite his fame, would not be invited. He was black.

In 1957, nine young blacks decided to challenge the unfair education system at Little Rock, Arkansas, which demanded separate provisions for blacks and whites. Despite threats and lengthy court proceedings, the young people won a great victory.

It is just over forty years ago that Martin Luther King dreamed his dream and was shot dead for doing so. He saw the promised land but died before he reached it. 'Strange Fruit' continues:

Pastoral scene of the gallant south,
The bulging eyes and the twisted mouth,
Scent of magnolias, sweet and fresh,
Then the sudden smell of the burning flesh.

Here is fruit for the crows to pluck,
For the rain to gather, for the wind to suck,
For the sun to rot, for the trees to drop,
Here is a strange and bitter crop.

Today, the poplar trees of the states of Mississippi, Alabama and are bare. No smell of burning human flesh wafts on the wind. Today, there is a black man sitting in the White House. Luther King's dream lives.

Forget the huge task that faces Barack Obama. He is there, and that is what matters. One of my most poignant experiences during my numerous visits to America was my invitation, with Dill, to a mass organised by Mary Lou Williams at St Ignatius Loyola's Church at Park Avenue and 84th Street on Good Friday during my first visit to New York back in 1973. Mary Lou Williams, a stride pianist, was regarded as the most influential woman in jazz. The mass was in the form of a liturgy, a thanksgiving service where instrumentalists and choirs came together to worship God and to thank him for the gift of jazz.

It was there that I heard the greatest tribute ever to the importance of jazz in people's lives. I still treasure the official programme printed for the occasion. And when someone asks me the meaning of jazz, I tend to quote from it. In it, jazz is presented as the inheritance of the people. 'Jazz', said Mary Lou Williams:

> is our American heritage. It is the only fully developed authentic art form created in America. It is our unique contribution to world culture. This music was born in suffering and from oppression – the suffering of American black people. It is from this suffering, at its origin, that this soulful music called jazz acquires that deep spiritual feeling and power that is healing to the soul. Jazz is a music created out of deep and soulful experience. It is music filled with

charity and love. It is also characterised by the creative process of improvisation, and, therefore by musical conversation among the instrumentalists involved in creating the music.

This music, more than any other, requires that the musicians be deeply involved with one another. Charity and love must flow from one to the other in order that the soulful feeling of good jazz be created. The moment a soloist's hands touch his instrument, ideas start to flow from the mind, through the heart and out the fingertips. At least, that is how it ought to be. Your attentive and prayerful participation, through listening through your ears and through your heart will allow you to enjoy fully this exchange of ideas, to sense these various moods and to reap the full therapeutic rewards that good music always brings to a tired, disturbed soul.

And that is the music and art that was brought to Llanelli by black American soldiers, the music that has enriched my life. Seventy years

Rosemary and me with our granddaughter Ffion and grandson Rhodri

since Billie Holiday sang 'Strange Fruit', an African-American man now occupies the White House as the first-ever black American President. It has been a long journey for the children of suffering. And jazz did its bit in leading the way in toppling the walls of prejudice. All I did was follow the band.